Bond
No.1 for exam success

English

Assessment Papers

10-11+ years

Book 2

OXFORD
UNIVERSITY PRESS

OXFORD
UNIVERSITY PRESS

Great Clarendon Street, Oxford, OX2 6DP, United Kingdom

Oxford University Press is a department of the University of Oxford.
It furthers the University's objective of excellence in research,
scholarship, and education by publishing worldwide. Oxford is a
registered trade mark of Oxford University Press in the UK and in
certain other countries

British Library Cataloguing in Publication Data
Data available

978-0-19-277739-3

10 9 8 7 6 5 4 3 2

Paper used in the production of this book is a natural, recyclable
product made from wood grown in sustainable forests.
The manufacturing process conforms to the environmental
regulations of the country of origin.

Printed in Great Britain by Ashford Colour Press Ltd.

Acknowledgements

The publishers would like to thank the following for permissions to
use copyright material:

Page make-up: OKS Prepress, India
Illustrations: Lisa Smith (Sylvie Poggio Artists Agency)
Cover illustrations: Lo Cole

Pp 3–4 extract from *Kensuke's Kingdom* by Michael Morpurgo, copyright © 1999
Michael Morpurgo. Published by Egmont Books, reproduced by permission of
David Higham Associates; pp9–10 'Greens never tasted so good' by Rebecca
Smithers, in the *Guardian* 21 November 2006. Copyright Guardian News and
Media Ltd 2006; p15 'George' from *Complete Verse* by Hilaire Belloc. Copyright
© The Estate of Hilaire Belloc 1970. Reproduced by Peters Fraser & Dunlop on
behalf of the Estate of Hilaire Belloc; pp27–28 'Captain Scott – Antarctic
Explorer', extract from the National Maritime Museum website; pp38–39
extract from *Long Walk to Freedom* by Nelson Mandela, Copyright © Nelson
Rolihlahla Mandela 2001. Reprinted by permission of Little, Brown and
Company; pp44–45 extract from *The No. 1 Ladies' Detective Agency* by Alexander
McCall Smith, copyright © Alexander McCall Smith 1999. Published by Birlinn,
reprinted by permissions of David Higham Associates; pp50–51 extract from
A Walk for Jim by Sally Thomas, Copyright © Sally Thomas 2001; pp57–58
extract from *Blitzcat* by Robert Westall © The Estate of Robert Westall 1994.
Published by HarperCollins, reprinted by permission of Laura Cecil Agency.

Although we have made every effort to trace and contact all
copyright holders before publication this has not been possible in all
cases. If notified, the publisher will rectify any errors or omissions at
the earliest opportunity.

Links to third party websites are provided by Oxford in good faith
and for information only. Oxford disclaims any responsibility for
the materials contained in any third party website referenced in
this work.

What is Bond?

This book is part of the Bond Assessment Papers series for English, which provides **thorough and continuous practice of key English skills** from ages five to thirteen. Bond's English resources are ideal preparation for Key Stage 1 and Key Stage 2 SATs, the 11+ and other selective school entrance exams.

How does the scope of this book match real exam content?

English 10-11+ Book 1 and *Book 2* are the core Bond 11+ books. Each paper is **pitched at the level of a typical 11+ exam** and practises comprehension, spelling, grammar and vocabulary work. The papers are also in line with other selective exams for this age group. The coverage is matched to the National Curriculum and the National Literacy Strategy and will also **provide invaluable preparation for Key Stage 2 SATs**. It is outside the scope of this book to practise extended and creative writing skills. *Bond Focus on Writing* provides full coverage of writing skills.

What does the book contain?

- **10 papers** – each one contains 100 questions.

- **Tutorial links throughout** – – this icon appears in the margin next to the questions. It indicates links to the relevant section in *How to do ... 11+ English*, our invaluable subject guide that offers explanations and practice for all core question types.

- **Scoring devices** – there are score boxes in the margins and a Progress Chart on page 64. The chart is a visual and motivating way for children to see how they are doing. It also turns the score into a percentage that can help decide what to do next.

- **Next Steps Planner** – advice on what to do after finishing the papers can be found on the inside back cover.

- **Answers** – located in an easily-removed central pull-out section.

How can you use this book?

One of the great strengths of Bond Assessment Papers is their flexibility. They can be used at home, in school and by tutors to:

- **set timed formal practice tests** – allow about 50 minutes per paper in line with standard 11+ demands. Reduce the suggested time limit by five minutes to practise working at speed

- provide **bite-sized chunks** for regular practice

- **highlight strengths and weaknesses** in the core skills

- identify **individual needs**

- set **homework**

- follow **a complete 11+ preparation strategy** alongside *The Parents' Guide to the 11+* (see below).

It is best to start at the beginning and work through the papers in order. If you are using the book as part of a careful run-in to the 11+, we suggest that you also have four other essential Bond resources close at hand:

Bond 11+ English Handbook: the subject guide that explains all the question types practised in this book. Use the cross-reference icons to find the relevant sections.

Focus on Comprehension: the practical handbook that clearly shows children how to read and understand the text, understand the questions and assess their own answers.

Focus on Writing: the essential resource that explains the key components of successful writing.

The Parents' Guide to the 11+: the step-by-step guide to the whole 11+ experience. It clearly explains the 11+ process, provides guidance on how to assess children, helps you to set complete action plans for practice and explains how you can use *English 10-11+ Book 1* and *Book 2* as part of a strategic run-in to the exam.

See the inside front cover for more details of these books.

What does a score mean and how can it be improved?

It is unfortunately impossible to guarantee that a child will pass the 11+ exam if they achieve a certain score on any practice book or paper. Success on the day depends on a host of factors, including the scores of the other children sitting the test. However, we can give some guidance on what a score indicates and how to improve it.

If children colour in the Progress Chart on page 64, this will give an idea of present performance in percentage terms. The Next Steps Planner inside the back cover will help you to decide what to do next to help a child progress. It is always valuable to go over wrong answers with children. If they are having trouble with any particular question type, follow the tutorial links to *How to do ... 11+ English* for step-by-step explanations and further practice.

Don't forget the website ...!

Visit www.bond11plus.co.uk for lots of advice, information and suggestions on everything to do with Bond, the 11+ and helping children to do their best.

Key words

Some special words are used in this book. You will find them in **bold** each time they appear in the Papers. These words are explained here.

abbreviation   a word or words which are shortened

abstract noun   a word referring to a concept or idea   *love*

active verb   when the main person or thing does the action   *he took it*

adjectival phrase   a group of words describing a noun

adjective   a word that describes somebody or something

adverb   a word that gives extra meaning to a verb

adverbial phrase   a word or phrase that makes the meaning of a verb, adjective or another adverb more specific, e.g. The Cheshire cat vanished *quite slowly*, beginning with the end of its tail

alphabetical order   words arranged in the order found in the alphabet

antonym   a word with a meaning opposite to another word   *hot – cold*

clause   a section of a sentence with a verb

collective noun   a word referring to a group   *swarm*

compound word   a word made up of two other words   *football*

conditional   a clause or sentence expressing the idea that one thing depends on another

conjunction   a word used to link sentences, phrases or words   *and, but*

connective   a word or words that join clauses or sentences

contraction   two words shortened into one with an apostrophe placed where the letter/s have been dropped   *do not = don't*

definition   meanings of words

diminutive   a word implying smallness   *booklet*

fronted adverbial   an adverbial that has been moved before the verb, e.g. *The day after tomorrow,* I'm going on holiday

homophone   words that have the same sound as another but a different meaning or spelling   *right/write*

indirect speech   (also known as reported speech) what has been said without using the exact words or inverted commas

main clause   a clause in a sentence which makes sense on its own

metaphor   a figurative expression in which something is described in terms usually associated with another   *the sky is a sapphire sea*

modal verb   verbs that change the meaning of other verbs, e.g. can, will

multi-clause sentence   a sentence made up of more than one clause

noun   a word for somebody or something

object   a noun referring to a person or thing which is affected by the action of a verb   *He ate an ice cream*

onomatopoeic   a word that echoes a sound, associated with its meaning   *hiss*

parenthesis   this is a word or phrase that is separated off from the main sentence by brackets, commas or dashes usually because it contains additional information not essential to its understanding

passive verb   when the main person or thing has the action done to it   *it was taken by him*

past tense   something that has already happened

phrase   a group of words that act as a unit

plural   more than one   *cats*

prefix   a group of letters added to the beginning of a word   *un, dis*

preposition   a word that relates other words to each other   *the book on the table*

pronoun   a word used to replace a noun

proper noun   the name of a person, place, etc.   *Ben*

relative clause	a special type of subordinate clause that makes the meaning of a noun more specific, e.g. The prize *that I won* was a book
root word	words to which prefixes or suffixes can be added to make other words *quick*ly
simile	an expression to describe what something is like *as cold as ice*
singular	one *cat*
subject	the person or thing who does the action expressed by the verb *the lion* roared
subordinate clause	gives more information about and is dependent on the main clause
suffix	a group of letters added to the end of a word *ly, ful*
superlative	describes the limit of a quality (adjective or adverb) *most/least* or *shortest*
synonym	a word with the same or very similar meaning to another word *quick – fast*
verb	a 'doing' or 'being' word

It is so dark out there. Black. Stella's barking. She's up by the bow. She hasn't got her harness clipped on.

Those were the last words I [Michael] ever wrote in my log. After that it's just empty pages.

I tried calling Stella first, but she wouldn't come. So I left the wheel and went   5
forward to bring her back. I took the ball with me to sweeten her in, tempt her away
from the bow of the boat.

I crouched down. 'Come on, Stella,' I said, rolling the ball from hand to hand.
'Come and get the ball.' I felt the boat turn a little in the wind, and I knew then I
shouldn't have left the wheel. The ball rolled away from me quite suddenly. I lunged   10
after it, but it was gone over the side before I could grab it. I lay there on the deck
watching it bob away into the darkness. I was furious with myself for being so silly.

I was still cursing myself when I thought I heard the sound of singing. Someone
was singing out there in the darkness. I called out but no one replied. So that was
what Stella had been barking at.   15

I looked again for my ball, but by now it had disappeared. That ball had been very
precious to me, precious to all of us. I knew then I had just lost a great deal more
than a football.

I was angry with Stella. The whole thing had been her fault. She was still barking. I
couldn't hear the singing any more. I called her again, whistled her in. She wouldn't   20
come. I got to my feet and went forward. I took her by the collar and pulled. She
would not be moved. I couldn't drag her all the way back, so I bent down to pick
her up. She was still reluctant. Then I had her in my arms, but she was struggling.

I heard the wind above me in the sails. I remember thinking: this is silly, you haven't
got your safety harness on, you haven't got your lifejacket on, you shouldn't be   25
doing this. Then the boat veered violently and I was thrown sideways. With my arms
full I had no time to grab the guard rail. We were in the cold of the sea before I
could even open my mouth to scream.

The terrors came fast, one upon another. The lights of the *Peggy Sue* went away
into the dark of the night, leaving me alone in the ocean, alone with the certainty   30
that they were already too far away, that my cries for help could not possibly be
heard. I thought then of the sharks cruising the black water beneath me – scenting
me, already searching me out, homing in on me – and I knew there could be no
hope. I would be eaten alive. Either that or I would drown slowly. Nothing could
save me.   35

I trod water, frantically searching the impenetrable darkness about me for
something, anything to swim towards. There was nothing.

Then a sudden glimpse of white in the sea. The breaking of a wave perhaps. But
there were no waves. Stella! It had to be. I was so thankful, so relieved not to be all
alone. I called out and swam towards her. She would keep bobbing away from   40
me, vanishing, reappearing, then vanishing again. She had seemed so near, but it

took several minutes of hard swimming before I came close enough to reach out and touch her. Only then did I realise my mistake. Stella's head was mostly black. This was white. It was my football. I grabbed it and clung on, feeling the unexpected and wonderful buoyancy of it. I held on, treading water and calling for Stella. There   *45* was no answer. I called and called. But every time I opened my mouth now, the seawater washed in. I had to give her up. I had to save myself if I could.

From *Kensuke's Kingdom* by Michael Morpurgo

Underline the correct answers.

1 Why was the log in the passage the last written by Michael?

(he couldn't think what else to write, his log book fell off the boat,

he fell off the boat)

2 Why did Michael take the ball to the bow of the boat?

(to coax Stella away from the bow, to play a game with Stella,

to put it out of the way)

3 Why does Michael think Stella was barking?

(she'd seen something in the water, she'd heard what she thought was singing,

she was playing a game with him)

③ 3

Answer these questions.

4–5 In lines 9–10 Michael states 'I knew then I shouldn't have left the wheel'. What made him think this and why?

_____

_____

6 What could the singing have been?

_____

7 Why was Michael angry with Stella?

_____

8 On falling in the water, what was Michael's biggest fear?

_____

9 What is the meaning of 'impenetrable' on line 36?

_____

10–12 Pick out three pieces of evidence that tell the reader how Michael felt after falling off the *Peggy Sue*.

_____

_____

_____

13 What sort of weather is suggested by the passage?

_____

14–15 Look again at the final sentence. Explain two ways you would go about doing this if you were in Michael's place.

_____

_____

12

D 9

Write a **synonym** for the words in bold.

16 The fence needed to be **strengthened**.   _____

17 The road was **blocked** with traffic.   _____

18 Will you **look after** my baby?   _____

19 The cheese was **ready to eat**.   _____

20 The **brother and sister** usually got on well.   _____

21 The constant howling wind made the dogs feel **anxious**.   _____

22 Her **description** of events was different.   _____

7

D 4

Add the missing commas to these sentences.

23–24 Plaster covered the lower part of his leg his foot his right arm and shoulder!

25–28 We had to walk down the hill catch the bus jump on a train take another bus and walk up the street just to get to Uncle Matt's house.

29–31 We were so excited we were having a picnic with crusty bread sandwiches glistening pork pies crunchy apples sparkling drinks and piles of chocolate bars.

9

E 2

Complete these words with *cious* or *tious*.

32 vi_____   **33** cau_____

34 mali_____   **35** ambi_____

36 nutri_____

37 pre_____

38 deli_____

39 suspi_____

In each space write the most suitable **adverb**. Each word may be used only once.

immediately   tearfully   thoroughly   frantically

hysterically   slowly   peacefully

40 The kittens slept _____ next to the open fire.

41 Nina felt _____ unwell.

42 The twins laughed _____ as their dad slipped in the mud.

43 The tower had been _____ toppling over for decades.

44 Wang Ling sat up, saw her new book by her bed and _____
started to read.

45 Ben _____ swam to the surface of the water.

46 As Bola's grandparents left he _____ said good-bye.

Circle the masculine words.

47–51

niece	ewe	lord	sow
boar	men	doe	bull
duke	wife		

Rewrite these sentences without double negatives.

52 There weren't no clouds in the sky.

_____

53 Kate hadn't done no homework.

_____

54 There isn't no water for the dog to drink.

_____

3

Write two sentences that indicate **parenthesis** using brackets, commas or dashes.

C 4

55 _____

_____

56 _____

_____

2

E 1

Write *their*, *there* or *they're* in each gap.

57–58 If we don't hurry _____ going to be late for _____ train.

59–60 _____ boots are _____.

61–63 Over _____ _____ working very hard on _____ paintings.

64–65 Look over _____, it looks like _____ cat has fallen in the pond!

9

D 5

Rewrite the passage correctly, starting a new line when a different person starts to speak.

66–82 Go and sit down both of you the teacher ordered But … I tried to explain as we made our way to our desks Now get on with your work the dreaded voice said No more cheating or insolence I want you to sit in your seats take out your books and start reading

_____

_____

_____

_____

_____

17

D 1

Write **active** or **passive** next to each sentence.

83 Ellen grabbed the ball and ran. _____

84 The cows walked slowly across the field. _____

85 Daniel was knocked out of the tree. _____

86 The cars raced around the track. _____

4

Add a **clause** to each of these to make a longer sentence. Use a different **conjunction** each time.

D 2
D 6

87–88 The water rose quickly, cutting off our exit _____

_____

89–90 The water rose quickly, cutting off our exit _____

_____

91–92 The water rose quickly, cutting off our exit _____

_____

6

Rewrite the misspelt words correctly.

E 2

93 parlament _____   **94** pronuncation _____

95 recomend _____   **96** musle _____

97 aparent _____   **98** comunicate _____

99 frequantly _____   **100** atached _____

8

Now go to the Progress Chart to record your score!   Total ◯ 100

8

Greens never tasted so good

Janet Parkinson, head of Howarth Primary School near Bradford, in Yorkshire, sums
up Steve Thorpe in just one word: 'He's … wow!' Steve, who has two daughters
at the school, works full-time as a gardener with the local council and nearly five
years ago set up an after-school gardening club at the school, initially as a way of
resolving some vandalism problems in the town.   5

Flowers and plants were grown and used to smarten up the town centre, and the
vandalism stopped. The project has gone from strength to strength and is now not
only central to food and other education in the school, but has led to closer links
with the local community.

Now 40 regular members of Steve's popular after-school gardening club (another   10
eager 20 pupils are on a waiting list) plant and tend the vegetables, while the whole
school (260 pupils plus 45 in the nursery) regularly gets involved in harvesting
the vegetables, shelling peas and peeling potatoes in the school kitchen and then
eating their efforts for their school lunches.

Over the past year, the range of vegetables served up at lunchtime has included   15
peas, tomatoes, lettuce, cucumber, peppers, runner beans, carrots, leeks, potatoes,
Brussels sprouts, cabbage and beetroot. Produce has been entered into local

horticultural shows – winning trophy after trophy for the youngsters. The school has won three 'Yorkshire in Bloom' plaudits.

Thorpe is now one of four individuals shortlisted for one of the Soil Association's prestigious annual school food awards, due to be presented on Thursday by chef Jamie Oliver and the association's school meals policy advisor, Jeanette Orrey, at a ceremony in Birmingham. 20

… The school food hero award recognises one individual who has worked hard to make a difference to school meals in their area. 25

Steve, now also a parent governor, is modest about his achievements. He says: 'For me the most satisfying part is the vegetable gardening, because now I feel that the whole school is involved, and growing is there in the curriculum, too. Many of these children thought vegetables came straight out of plastic bags, not the ground.' The community has also benefited, and the grateful local police have donated plant-pots, because the gardening club maintains their flowers. 30

If Steve wins the award, the school will receive £1,000. And his priority for the money? It has been earmarked to pay for the much-needed extension of the school's greenhouse …

From an article in the *Guardian* by Rebecca Smithers

Underline the correct answers.

1 How long has the school gardening club been running?

(less than five years, five years, more than five years)

2 How many children are or would like to be involved in the school gardening club?

(40, 45, 60)

3 The school food hero award is provided by which organisation?

(Yorkshire County Council, The Soil Association, Howarth Primary School) ◖ 3

Answer these questions.

4 Why is Janet Parkinson so impressed with Steve Thorpe?

_____

5–7 Detail three benefits the gardening club has had for Howarth Primary School.

_____

_____

_____

8 Why do you think the planting of flowers and plants in the town centre helped stop the vandalism?

_____

9 What does the **phrase** 'the project has gone from strength to strength' mean (line 7)?

_____

10 Give the meaning of the word 'plaudits' (line 19) as it is used in the passage.

_____

11–12 Why is this school club about more than just the children growing and eating their own vegetables? Give two reasons.

_____

_____

13 Why do you think an extension is needed for the club's greenhouse?

_____

14–15 List two of Steve's characteristics that make him popular with both children and teachers.

_____

_____

12

E 2

Add the **suffix** _ive_ to each of these words. Don't forget any spelling changes.

16 conduct _____   **17** invent _____

18 progress _____   **19** cooperate _____

20 speculate _____   **21** alternate _____

22 impress _____   **23** offence _____

8

D 4

Add the missing commas to these sentences.

24–25 Steven watched in slow motion as the ball flew towards the house just missing the garden statue skimmed the rose bushes and smashed through the kitchen window

26–27 The voice a man's voice was deep and powerful though at times very quiet.

28–30 Steven watched in slow motion as the ball flew towards the house just missing the neighbour's cat skimmed the flowers gently rocking the garden statue and smashed the kitchen window!

7

Write two **adjectives** to describe each of these **nouns**. A different word must be used each time.

D 6

31–32 _____, _____ dog

33–34 _____, _____ whistle

35–36 _____, _____ tree

6

Write two sentences that include a **relative clause** using the following words.

37 where

_____

38 who

_____

2

Write two meanings for each of these words. One might be a meaning that has evolved over recent years.

39–40 paddy

_____

_____

41–42 green

_____

_____

4

With a line, match the beginning of the proverb with its end.

C 4

43 More haste,   without fire.

44 First come,   in one basket.

45 There is no smoke   less speed.

46 Don't put all your eggs   flock together.

47 Birds of a feather   has a silver lining.

48 Every cloud   first served.

6

Choose the correct **verb** form for each of these sentences.

D 6

49 Damien (is/are) best friends with Tom and Reuben.

50 The friends were loving the theme park.

51 Veejay could (saw/see) that the beans had been growing.

52 Sarah (catched/caught) the ball confidently.

53 Mitchell found the homework (what/that) he'd been looking for.

54 Helen (turned/turning) her head away instinctively.

55 There (was/were) no moon and they couldn't see much.

7

Add the **suffix** to each of these words. Don't forget any spelling changes.

E 2

56 consider + able _____   57 notice + able _____

58 measure + able _____   59 response + ible _____

60 reproduce + ible _____   61 access + ible _____

62 reason + able _____   63 change + able _____

8

Punctuate these sentences correctly.

D 5

64–69 that film terrified me gulped danny

_____

70–76 meena slipped down into the fast moving river help she screamed

_____

77–86 let's eat our lunch here said jay it's warm in the sun

_____

23

Finish these **similes**, using your own words.

C 4

87 as shiny as _____

88 as black as _____

89 as fast as a _____

90 as strong as _____

4

Rewrite these statements as questions, changing as few words as possible.

91 There are fewer people in Australia than in the United Kingdom.

_____

92 We are going to the party tonight.

_____

Add a **prefix** to each of these to make a new word.

93 _____social   **94** _____normal

95 _____act   **96** _____scope

97 _____polite   **98** _____connect

99 _____operate   **100** _____circle

When George's Grandmamma was told
That George had been as good as Gold,
She Promised in the Afternoon
To buy him an *Immense BALLOON*.
And   5
so she did; but when it came,
It got into a candle flame,
And being of a dangerous sort
Exploded
with a loud report!   10
The Lights went out! The Windows broke!
The Room was filled with reeking smoke.
And in the darkness shrieks and yells
Were mingled with Electric Bells,
And falling masonry and groans,   15
And crunching, as of broken bones,
And dreadful shrieks, when, worst of all,
The House itself began to fall!
It tottered, shuddering to and fro,
Then crashed into the street below –   20
Which happened to be Savile Row.
When Help arrived, among the Dead
Were
Cousin Mary,
Little Fred,   25
The Footmen
(both of them),
The Groom,
The man that cleaned the Billiard Room,
The Chaplain, and   30
The Still-Room Maid.
And I am dreadfully afraid
That Monsieur Champignon, the Chef,
Will now be
permanently deaf –   35
And both his
Aides
are much the same
While George, who was in part to blame,
Received, you will regret to hear,   40
A nasty lump
behind the ear.

MORAL
The moral is that little Boys
Should not be given dangerous Toys.   45

George by Hilaire Belloc

15

Underline the correct answers.

1 Why was George given the balloon?

(for being strong and bold, for doing what he was told,

for being as good as gold)

2 What happened to Monsieur Champignon?

(he died, he received a nasty lump, he became deaf)

Answer these questions.

3 What is the meaning of the word 'Immense' on line 4?

_____

4–6 When the balloon exploded it triggered a number of events. List six of them.

_____

_____

_____

7 The poem states that George was 'in part to blame' (line 39). Why?

_____

8–10 As you read the poem you will notice that some words or **phrases** have been presented by the poet in different ways. Write two ways the poet has done this and explain why this has been done.

_____

_____

11–12 What message does the poem convey? Do you think the message is just?

_____

_____

13–15 Describe two ways the poet wanted the readers to feel when reading the poem. Use one piece of evidence from the poem to support your answer.

_____

_____

_____

In each sentence underline the **object** and write a **pronoun** for each **subject**.

D 7

16–17 The children played in the pool.   subject pronoun _____

18–19 The baby slept in the cot.   subject pronoun _____

20–21 Henry rode his bike to school.   subject pronoun _____

22–23 The firemen relaxed after putting out the fire. subject pronoun _____

8

From the **verbs** listed write a **noun** ending in *ion*.

D 6

24 divide	_____	25 invade	_____
26 explode	_____	27 rotate	_____
28 collide	_____	29 comprehend	_____
30 confess	_____	31 deflect	_____

8

Use each word in a sentence to show its meaning. You can add **suffixes** to them.

E 2

32 dextrous _____

33 conceit _____

34 exhilarate _____

35 persistence _____

36 pursue _____

37 yield _____

6

Write the two words each **contraction** stands for.

D 5

38 we're _____ _____

39 should've _____ _____

40 I'll _____ _____

41 won't _____ _____

42 let's _____ _____

43 shan't _____ _____

6

Write six sentences. In each sentence use the listed phrase correctly.

44 heavy metal detector

_____

45 heavy-metal detector

_____

46 hot water bottle

_____

47 hot-water bottle

_____

48 man eating crocodile

_____

49 man-eating crocodile

_____

D 6
6

Write an **antonym** for each of these words.

D 9

50 subtract _____   **51** scream _____

52 extend _____   **53** least _____

54 spectator _____   **55** confident _____

56 mend _____   **57** exterior _____

8

In each of these sentences a word is incorrect. Underline the word and rewrite it correctly.

D 13

58 The Stamp family can't move until the removal truck was here.

_____

59 Kyle and me went swimming.

_____

60 Darren, Wusai and I is a good team.

_____

61 The paint weren't drying quickly enough.

_____

62 Najib didn't want no tea.

_____

5

Underline the **root words** in each of these.

63 transmigrate   **64** reintroduce   **65** intersection

66 debater   **67** consistent   **68** resistance

69 antifreeze   **70** almighty

Copy these sentences, adding the missing punctuation and capital letters.

71–82 quick called laura if we hurry we can catch the bus from waterloo road

_____

_____

83–89 come on then shouted anna as she raced off

_____

Complete the second **clause** (that includes a **verb**) for each of these sentences.

90 I read a book each night that _____

_____

91 My mum takes the bus to work _____

_____

92 I ate my supper while _____

_____

Write the **plural** form of these words.

93 waltz   _____   **94** glass   _____

95 chief   _____   **96** scenario   _____

97 identity   _____   **98** success   _____

99 werewolf   _____   **100** quiz   _____

Now go to the Progress Chart to record your score!   Total   100

19

The train had stopped before a red signal which blocked the way. The engineer and conductor were talking excitedly with a signal-man, whom the station-master at Medicine Bow, the next stopping place, had sent on before. The passengers drew around and took part in the discussion, in which Colonel Proctor, with his insolent manner, was conspicuous. 5

Passepartout, joining the group, heard the signal-man say, 'No! you can't pass. The bridge at Medicine Bow is shaky, and would not bear the weight of the train.'

This was a suspension-bridge thrown over some rapids, about a mile from the place they now were. According to the signal-man, it was in a ruinous condition, several of the iron wires being broken; and it was impossible to risk the passage. 10 He did not in any way exaggerate the condition of the bridge.

Passepartout, not daring to apprise his master of what he heard, listened with set teeth, immovable as a statue.

'Hum!' cried Colonel Proctor; 'but we are not going to stay here, I imagine, and take root in the snow?' 15

'Colonel,' replied the conductor, 'we have telegraphed to Omaha for a train, but it is not likely that it will reach Medicine Bow in less than six hours.'

'Six hours!' cried Passepartout.

'Certainly,' returned the conductor. 'Besides, it will take us as long as that to reach Medicine Bow on foot.' 20

'But it is only a mile from here,' said one of the passengers.

'Yes, but it's on the other side of the river.'

'And can't we cross that in a boat?' asked the colonel.

'That's impossible. The creek is swelled by the rains. It is a rapid, and we shall have to make a circuit of ten miles to the north to find a ford.' 25

The colonel launched a volley of oaths, denouncing the railway company and the conductor; and Passepartout, who was furious, was not disinclined to make common cause with him. Here was an obstacle, indeed, which all his master's bank-notes could not remove …

Passepartout found that he could not avoid telling his master what had occurred, and, with hanging head, he was turning towards the car when the engineer … – named Forster – called out, 'Gentlemen, perhaps there is a way, after all, to get over.' 30

'On the bridge?' asked a passenger.

'On the bridge.'

'With our train?' 35

'With our train.'

Passepartout stopped short, and eagerly listened to the engineer.

'But the bridge is unsafe,' urged the conductor.

'No matter,' replied Forster; 'I think that by putting on the very highest speed we might have a chance of getting over.' 40

'The devil!' muttered Passepartout.

But a number of the passengers were at once attracted by the engineer's proposal, and Colonel Proctor was especially delighted, and found the plan a very feasible one. He told stories about engineers leaping their trains over rivers without bridges, by putting on full steam; and many of those present avowed themselves of 45 the engineer's mind.

Passepartout was astounded, and, though ready to attempt anything to get over Medicine Creek, thought the experiment proposed a little too American. 'Besides,' thought he, 'there's a still more simple way, and it does not even occur to any of these people! Sir,' said he aloud to one of the passengers, 'the engineer's plan 50 seems to me a little dangerous, but –' …

'Are you afraid?' asked Colonel Proctor.

'I afraid! Very well; I will show these people that a Frenchman can be as American as they!'

'All aboard!' cried the conductor. 55

'Yes, all aboard!' repeated Passepartout, and immediately. 'But they can't prevent me from thinking that it would be more natural for us to cross the bridge on foot, and let the train come after!'

But no one heard this sage reflection, nor would anyone have acknowledged its justice … 60

The locomotive whistled vigorously; the engineer, reversing the steam, backed the train for nearly a mile – retiring, like a jumper, in order to take a longer leap. Then, with another whistle, he began to move forward; the train increased its speed, and soon its rapidity became frightful; a prolonged screech issued from the locomotive; the piston worked up and down twenty strokes to the second. They 65 perceived that the whole train, rushing on at the rate of a hundred miles an hour, hardly bore upon the rails at all.

And they passed over! It was like a flash. No one saw the bridge. The train leaped, so to speak, from one bank to the other, and the engineer could not stop it until it had gone five miles beyond the station. But scarcely had the train passed 70 the river, when the bridge, completely ruined, fell with a crash into the rapids of Medicine Bow.

From *Around the World in Eighty Days* by Jules Verne

Underline the correct answers.

1 Why were the engineer and conductor talking 'excitedly'?

(because the train had broken down, because the bridge wasn't safe to cross,

because the bridge had collapsed)

2 What were the weather conditions like?

(snowy, rainy, sunny)

3 What nationality was Passepartout?

(American, British, French)

3

Answer these questions.

4 What is Medicine Bow?

_____

5 The author describes the suspension bridge as being 'thrown over some rapids'. What does he mean by this?

_____

6–8 Give the meaning of the following words as they are used in the passage.

insolent (line 4)   _____

sage (line 59)   _____

perceived (line 66)   _____

9 What is meant by the **phrase** 'was not disinclined to make common cause with him' (line 27)?

_____

10–11 What is meant by 'and many of those present avowed themselves of the engineer's mind' (line 45)? Why is this significant?

_____

_____

12 What evidence in the passage is there that the group discussed the issues off the train?

_____

13 What is the train likened to in line 62?

_____

14–15 How would you describe the sort of person Colonel Proctor is, as shown in the passage? Use evidence to support your answer.

_____

_____

12
E 1

Add *ie* or *ei* to each of these to make a word.

16 p___rce	**17** br___f	**18** conc___ve
19 f___nt	**20** w___gh	**21** dec___ve
22 retr___ve	**23** fr___ght	**24** dec___t

9
D 6

Add a different **conjunction** to each of these sentences.

25 The animals were frightened _____ the thunder and lightning passed above them.

26 Jacob picked up his coat slowly _____ the dogs began to circle him.

27 Shahida waited for the bus _____ it started to get dark.

28 The children ran and jumped into the stream _____ they felt so hot.

29 Fran desperately wanted to meet her friends at the bike park _____ she couldn't find her helmet.

5
C 4

Complete each sentence as a **metaphor**.

30 The moon is a _____.

31 The dress is a _____.

32 The fog was a _____.

33 The fireworks were _____.

34 The sleeping cat is a _____.

35 The crashing waves are _____.

6
D 5

Copy this sentence, adding the missing punctuation and capital letters.

36–50 tom are you awake whispered emily i can't find the torch ive brought and im scared

_____

_____

_____

15

Add a **suffix** to each word.

ship   ness   hood   less

51 neighbour   _____

52 defence   _____

53 friend   _____

54 kind   _____

55 scarce   _____

56 doubt   _____

57 space   _____

E 2

7

Rewrite each of the following, using only two words, one of which should have an apostrophe.

58 ward reserved for men   _____

59 ball for a dog   _____

60 wheel of a car   _____

61 stable for a pony   _____

62 toy belonging to the puppy   _____

D 5

5

Match a word in each column to make a **compound word**.

week   pot
no   out
land   will
jack   end
print   let
in   mark
on   where
good   going

63 _____   64 _____

65 _____   66 _____

67 _____   68 _____

69 _____   70 _____

D 11

8

When do the events in these sentences happen? Write **past**, **present** or **future**.

71 Sally fell off her bike. _____

72 The snow is covering the ground. _____

73 We went to Windsor Castle. _____

74 Melinda will have her flute lesson this afternoon. _____

75 The chicken pecks at the food. _____

76 The fireworks display will be at 7pm. _____

77 It rained when Uncle James got married. _____

Write two comparing **phrases** using each of these words.

Example: cautious   *less cautious,   more cautious*

78–79 reliable _____

_____

80–81 manageable _____

_____

82–83 visible _____

_____

Circle the unstressed vowel in each of these words.

84 u s u a l l y   85 l i s t e n e r   86 b u s i n e s s

87 p e t a l   88 v a l u a b l e   89 t r a v e l l e r

90 c h o c o l a t e   91 d e s p e r a t e   92 h i s t o r y

Put these words in **alphabetical order**.

93–97 impoverish   (1) _____

impossible   (2) _____

important   (3) _____

impracticable   (4) _____

imposition   (5) _____

D 6

7

D 2

6

E 2

9

5

25

Write an interesting paragraph that makes use of bullet points. Write about a hobby you have.

98–100

3

Captain Scott – Antarctic explorer

Until the end of the 19th century, only sealers and whalers had set foot on the desolate southern land we call Antarctica. Until as late as 1820, no one had even seen its mainland. In the 1890s however, explorers of various countries began to compete for being the first to reach both the North and the South Poles. In 1901–04 Captain Robert Falcon Scott (1868–1912), an officer in the Royal Navy, was the first   5 person to explore Antarctica extensively by land.

Was Britain the only country trying to reach the South Pole?

No. Several expeditions from Norway, France and Germany explored Antarctica. While Scott was sailing south on his second expedition, he heard the news that the Norwegian, Roald Amundsen, was going to Antarctica and was likely to reach the   10 South Pole first. Although Amundsen was an experienced Arctic explorer, Scott was determined to get there first. He laid food depots to the south early in 1911, and set out towards the Pole on 1 November during the second summer there.

What happened on the second expedition?

Scott planned to reach the Pole from Ross Island, using ponies and three motorised   *15*
sledges, with a few dogs in support, then by man-hauling his sledges. The
motorised sledges failed. The ponies suffered and were put down for food (which
was expected) and the dogs went back to base camp halfway with most of the
men. This left Scott and just four companions to pull.

Did they reach the Pole?   *20*

Yes, they got there on 17–18 January 1912. When they arrived they found that
Amundsen and his four Norwegian companions had got there before them. Scott's
men had been beaten and, along with all the hardships of the return journey, their
morale was badly affected.

Had the two parties approached the Pole using different methods?   *25*

Yes, Amundsen made his base and set off from the 'Bay of Whales', on the ice-shelf
itself. This was about 100 km nearer to the Pole than Scott on Ross Island. The
Norwegians were experienced skiers and dog-drivers, who moved very fast using
52 dogs, in teams, to pull their sledges of food and essential equipment. Amundsen
also laid more depots in advance, and further south than Scott, and small ones as   *30*
he went. As his sledges became lighter he killed dogs to feed the others (and his
men). The British pulled the sledges themselves. Scott, who knew little about the
proper use of skis or dogs, believed this was more noble. While the Norwegians'
only aim was to reach the Pole first, Scott also made scientific observations and
collected rock samples on the way.   *35*

How far did they need to travel back to reach safety?

Scott and his party needed to return across the 800 miles they had already covered.
They had to get back before the middle of April, before the Antarctic winter brought
deadly freezing temperatures and constant darkness.

What happened to them?   *40*

They had a disastrous time. Terrible weather included blizzards and gale force
winds. They had only limited and poor food, and shortage of fuel. Eventually,
they all died. Evans died first, probably after knocking his head during a fall into a
crevasse. Oates knew he was suffering from severe frostbite in his feet, could not
go on, and did not want to slow the others down. On 17 March 1912, he left the   *45*
tent during a blizzard. His final words, written down by Scott, were: 'I am just going
outside, and I may be some time'. He was never seen again. The other three died
in their tent during a blizzard at the end of March. They were only 11 miles from the
food and fuel depot.

The bodies of Scott, Dr Wilson and 'Birdie' Bowers were found on 12 November.   *50*
They were in their sleeping bags inside a tent covered in snow. Their journals and
papers were recovered but the bodies were left, wrapped in a tent and buried under
a snow cairn.

Underline the correct answers.

1 How many expeditions did Scott make to Antarctica?

(one, two, three)

2 Which was Amundsen's native country?

(Norway, Germany, France)

3 Who got to the South Pole first?

(Scott, Amundsen, they reached it together)

○ 3

Answer these questions.

4 Describe the term 'man-hauling' (line 16).

_____

5–6 In your own words describe the type of place Antarctica is.

_____

_____

7–9 Name three things Amundsen did differently that ultimately made the difference in his attempt to reach the South Pole first.

_____

_____

_____

10 Why did Scott have to return before the middle of April?

_____

11–12 Describe the sort of person Amundsen was. Use evidence from the passage to support your answer.

_____

_____

13 With reference to the first two paragraphs only, what clue do we have that Captain Scott never made it back from Antarctica?

_____

14 How did we learn about Scott's exploration of Antarctica?

_____

15 When Oates left Scott's tent on 17 March 1912 he said 'I am just going outside, and I may be some time' (lines 46–47). Why do you think he said this?

_____

12

E 2

Each of these words has an unstressed vowel missing. Rewrite the words correctly.

16 machinry _____ **17** favourte _____

18 memry _____ **19** jewellry _____

20 impatent _____ **21** misrable _____

22 busness _____

7

E 2

Rewrite these sentences changing them from **singular** to **plural**.

23–26 The girl was riding her horse.

_____

27–29 The rabbit fled down its burrow.

_____

30–33 He saved a stamp to add to his collection.

_____

11

D 10

For the following **abbreviations**, write out the words in full.

34 DIY_____

35 p & p_____

36 Dr_____

3

D 6

Write the **nouns** in the correct columns of the table.

37–44 happiness   grass   opinion   team

gang   Harry   flame   December

common nouns	collective nouns	proper nouns	abstract nouns

8

Some questions will be answered in the children's own words. Answers to these questions are given in *italics*. Any answers that seem to be in line with these should be marked correct.

Paper 1 (pages 3–8)

1 **he fell off the boat** (line 25)
2 **to coax Stella away from the bow** (lines 6–7)
3 **she'd heard what she thought was singing** (lines 13–15)
4–5 *Michael thought that he shouldn't have left the wheel because he felt the boat start to turn in the wind. He was worried that he might get into trouble because if the wind started to move the boat, he wasn't at the wheel to steer it.*
6 *It could have been the wind.*
7 *He blamed her for the loss of his ball because if she hadn't been at the bow he wouldn't have been trying to get her back with it.* (lines 16–19)
8 **sharks** (lines 32–34)
9 *unable to see into or through*
10–12 *Michael felt a range of emotions. Firstly terror: 'The terrors came fast, one upon another.' (line 29) He also felt alone and on discovering what he thought was Stella he was 'so relieved not to be all alone' (lines 39–40). Finally he felt determined: 'I had to save myself if I could' (line 47). He didn't want to drown.*
13 *The weather is calm with the occasional stronger gust of wind.*
14–15 Child's answer suggesting ways to conserve energy, stay warm, not alert sharks and keep awake, e.g. *I would hold onto the ball because it would help me float without using up too much of my energy. I would try to determine where the boat might be and try to move in that direction.*
16–22 A synonym is a word that has the same, or similar, meaning to another word. For example, 'gigantic' is a synonym of 'large'. Here are some possible answers:
16 *reinforced*
17 *congested*
18 *mind*
19 *ripe*
20 *siblings*
21 *uneasy*
22 *version*
23–31 Commas are used to separate items in a list. No comma is needed between the last two items in the list, only the word 'and'. For example: *I went to the shop to buy some bread, eggs, butter and milk; or I packed some toothpaste, an extra blanket and some paperback books.*
23–24 Hard white plaster covered the lower part of his leg, his foot, his right arm and shoulder!
25–28 We had to walk down the hill, catch the bus, jump on a train, take another bus and walk up the street, just to get to Uncle Matt's house.
29–31 We were so excited we were having a picnic with crusty bread sandwiches, glistening pork pies, crunchy apples, sparkling drinks and piles of chocolate bars.
32–39 To help decide which suffix to add (refer to Paper 2 Q16–23 on suffixes), think of the root word (refer to Paper 5 Q62–69 on root words). If the root word ends in 'tion', this is replaced with 'tious'; if the root word ends in 'ce', this is replaced with 'cious'. The root words have been given below wherever possible.
32 **vicious** There is no root word for this word to help decide which suffix to add, so this spelling needs to be learnt individually.
33 **cautious** The root word is 'caution' 'tion' is removed and 'tious' is added.
34 **malicious** The root word is 'malice' so 'ce' is removed and 'cious' is added.
35 **ambitious** The root word is 'ambition' so 'tion' is removed and 'tious' is added.
36 **nutritious** The root word is 'nutrition' so 'tion' is removed and 'tious' is added.
37 **precious**
38 **delicious**
39 **suspicious** The root word is 'suspicion' so 'cion' is removed and 'cious' is added.
40–46 An adverb is a word that describes a verb; it describes how something has happened or how something is done.
40 The kittens slept **peacefully** next to the open fire.
41 Nina felt **thoroughly** unwell.
42 The twins laughed **hysterically** as their dad slipped in the mud.
43 The tower had been **slowly** toppling over for decades.
44 Wang Ling sat up, saw her new book by her bed and **immediately** started to read.
45 Ben **frantically** swam to the surface of the water.
46 As Bola's grandparents left he **tearfully** said good-bye.
47–51 **lord, boar, men, bull, duke**
52–54 A double negative is when two words meaning 'no' are used in a sentence, which makes its meaning confusing or unclear.

52 **There weren't any clouds in the sky.** 'Were no' can be used in place of 'weren't any'.

53 **Kate hadn't done any homework.**

54 **There isn't any water for the dog to drink.** 'Is no' can be used in place of 'isn't any'.

55–56 A parenthesis is a word or phrase that has been inserted into a sentence. If it is removed, the sentence will still make sense without it. The parenthesis will have either commas, brackets or dashes directly before and after it. For example: *The books, which were new, were left on the bus; The books (which were new) were left on the bus; The books – which were new – were left on the bus.*

57–65 These words are homophones. They sound the same but are spelled differently. 'There' tells us where something is; 'their' tells us who or what something belongs to; 'they're' is a short form of 'they are'.

57–58 **they're, their** If we don't hurry they're going to be late for their train.

59–60 **Their, there** Their boots are over there.

61–63 **there, they're, their** Over there they're working very hard on their paintings.

64–65 **there, their** Look over there, it looks like their cat has fallen in the pond!

66–82 'Go and sit down, both of you!' the teacher ordered.
'But...' I tried to explain as we made our way to our desks.
'Now get on with your work,' the dreaded voice said. 'No more cheating or insolence! I want you to sit in your seats, take out your books and start reading.'

83–86 A verb is an 'action' word, e.g. talked, ate, ran, an 'occurance', e.g. happen or a 'state', e.g. become. The verb in a sentence is active when the subject is completing the action, e.g. *The boy rode the horse.* The 'boy' is the subject and the action is 'rode'. In a passive sentence the subject has the action done to it, e.g. *The horse was ridden by the boy.* Passive verbs are usually preceded by 'was' or 'were', therefore 'was ridden' tells us the sentence is passive.

83 **active**

84 **active**

85 **passive**

86 **active**

87–92 A noun is a person, place or thing. A clause is a group of words that includes a subject (a noun or pronoun that is performing the verb) and a verb. Conjunctions are words that join two clauses together, e.g. *but, because, when,* etc. A possible answer is: *'The water rose quickly, cutting off our exit, so we turned around and went back the way we'd come.'*

93 **parliament**

94 **pronunciation**

95 **recommend**

96 **muscle**

97 **apparent**

98 **communicate**

99 **frequently**

100 **attached**

Paper 2 (pages 9–14)

1 **less than five years** (lines 3–4)

2 **60** (lines 10–11)

3 **The Soil Association** (lines 20–21)

4 *because of the huge impact he has made in her school*

5–7 *eating the food they have grown* (line 14); *winning trophies thus raising the school profile* (line 17–19); *providing an interesting way of learning about food* (line 29); *closer links with the local community* (lines 8–9)

8 *By improving the look of the town centre it has encouraged the young people to feel proud of their surroundings and therefore have less desire to vandalise it.*

9 *It continues to grow and each new task it undertakes is done well.*

10 *expressions of approval, awards*

11–12 *It has also benefited the community by taking responsibility for flower displays and care around the town. It has helped to stop vandalism in the town.* (lines 6–7)

13 *Due to the fact that the club is so popular and its activities are increasing, more room is needed for the additional plants that are being cared for.*

14–15 Answers might include his enthusiasm, his knowledge, his commitment, his modesty and his generosity.

16–23 A root word is the most basic form of a word which is able to have a prefix or suffix added to it. A suffix is a group of letters that are added to the end of a word; in this case the suffix is 'ive'. If the root word ends in a consonant then 'ive' just needs to be added (refer to Paper 5 Q62–69 on root words). If the root word ends in a silent 'e' then the 'e' is removed and 'ive' is added. If the root word ends in a soft 'c' sound, 'ce' needs to be replaced with 'sive'.

16 **conductive** The root word ends in a consonant so 'ive' just needs to be added.

17 **inventive**

18 **progressive**

19 **cooperative** The root word ends in a silent 'e' so this is removed and 'ive' is added.

20 **speculative**

A2

21 **alternative**
22 **impressive**
23 **offensive** The root word ends in a soft 'ce' so this is removed and replaced with 'sive'.
24–30 Refer to Paper 1 Q 23–31 and 55–56 on commas and parentheses.
24–25 The air caught unpleasantly in his throat, nearly making him cough, then struggled into his lungs.
25–27 The voice, a man's voice, was deep and powerful, though at times very quiet.
28–30 Steven watched in slow motion as the ball flew towards the house, just missing the neighbour's cat, skimming the flowers, gently rocking the garden statue and smashed the kitchen window!
31–36 An adjective is a word that gives more information about a noun (a person, place or thing), such as *yellow, large, excited,* or *sweet.* Here are some possible answers:
31–32 *shaggy, wet*   33–34 *shrill, loud*
35–36 *tall, majestic*
37–38 A relative clause gives you extra information about the noun or verb it relates to (refer to Paper 1 Q87–92 on nouns and Paper 1 Q83–86 on verbs). The sentence needs to include the relative pronoun given in each question, e.g. *'That is the school* **where** *my friend goes.'* or *'That's the girl* **who** *lives near my friend.'*
39–40 paddy – *a field where rice is grown; a rage or temper*
41–42 green – *a colour; environmentally friendly; inexperienced*
43–48 A proverb is a short saying that usually gives advice.
43 **More haste, less speed.**
44 **First come, first served.**
45 **There is no smoke without fire.**
46 **Don't put all your eggs in one basket.**
47 **Birds of a feather flock together.**
48 **Every cloud has a silver lining.**
49–55 Refer to Paper 1 Q83–86
49 Damien **is** best friends with Tom and Reuben.
50 The friends **were** loving the theme park.
51 Veejay could **see** that the beans had been growing.
52 Sarah **caught** the ball confidently.
53 Mitchell found the homework **which** he'd been looking for.
54 Helen **turned** her head away instinctively.
55 There **was** no moon and they couldn't see much.
56–63 The suffix 'able' is used if the complete root word can be heard after the suffix is added;

'ible' is used if the complete root cannot be heard. However, there are exceptions to this rule. Usually, if the words ends in a consonant followed by an 'e', the 'e' is removed and the suffix added. However, if the word ends in a soft 'c' (such as in *notice, place*) or soft 'g' (such as *dislodge, discharge*) then the 'e' needs to be kept and the suffix is just added.
56 **considerable** The suffix 'able' just needs to be added.
57 **noticeable** 'notice' ends in a 'soft c' so 'able' just needs to be added.
58 **measureable** This is an exception to the rule and 'able' just needs to be added.
59 **responsible** 'response' ends in a consonant followed by an 'e', so the 'e' is removed and the suffix is added.
60 **reproducible** This is an exception to the rule: 'e' is removed and 'ible' is added.
61 **accessible** The suffix 'ible' just needs to be added.
62 **reasonable**
63 **changeable** 'change' ends in a 'soft g' so 'able' just needs to be added.
64–69 'That film terrified me,' gulped Danny.
70–76 Meena slipped down into the fast moving river. 'Help!' she screamed.
77–86 'Let's eat our lunch here,' said Jay. 'It's warm in the sun.'
87–90 A simile is a phrase that compares one thing to another, in this case using the word 'as'. It is used to give a more detailed description, so the comparisons need to be appropriate. Here are some possible answers:
87 *as shiny as a jewel*
88 *as black as night*
89 *as fast as a cheetah*
90 *as strong as an iron bar*
91 **Are there fewer people in Australia than in the United Kingdom?**
92 **Are we going to the party tonight?**
93–100 A prefix is a small group of letters added to the beginning of a word which adjust the meaning, e.g. 'pre'; 'non', 're', etc. When a prefix is added, the spelling of the original word does not need to change. Here are some possible answers:
93 *antisocial*
94 *abnormal*
95 *interact*
96 *microscope*
97 *impolite*
98 *disconnect*
99 *co-operate*
100 *semicircle*

1 **for being as good as gold** (line 2)
2 **he became deaf** (lines 33–35)
3 *huge*
4–6 Acceptable answers could include the following events (2 events = 1 mark): *the lights went out; windows broke; smoke filled the room; people shrieked; loud bells sounded; masonry fell; bones were broken; the house fell down*
7 *because it was George's balloon that triggered the explosion when it came near the candle (lines 7–9)*
8–10 *The poet has used capital letters on unexpected words; italics; and new lines. The poet has done this to emphasise the words (to make them stand out).*
11–12 *The message of the poem is that boys shouldn't be given dangerous toys, which is right, but a balloon isn't normally classed as a dangerous toy!*
13–15 *The poet wanted readers to be shocked because the topic of the poem, an explosion leading to people dying, is serious. This is shown by the detailed list of the effects of the explosion as well as the list of people who died. The tone of the poem is, however, light so the poet also wanted people to be amused. This is shown in the way the people who died are named, such as 'little Fred'.*
16–23 The subject of the sentence is the noun/pronoun that is performing the verb. It often comes before the verb. The object in the sentence is the noun/pronoun that the verb is acting upon. It is often after the verb.
16–17 **pool, They** The object is the pool. The children are the subject so the pronoun is They.
18–19 **cot, He/She** The object is the cot. The subject is the baby so the pronoun is He or She.
20–21 **bike, He** The object is the bike. The subject is Henry so the pronoun is He.
22–23 **fire, They** The object is the fire. The firemen are the subject so the pronoun is They.
24–31 Refer to Paper 1 Q83–86 on verbs and Paper 1 Q87–92 on nouns. When adding the suffix 'ion', check to see which letters the word ends in. If it ends in 'te' or 't' then these are removed and 'tion' is added. If the word given ends in 'de', 'd', 's' or 'se' then these are removed and 'sion' is added. If the word ends in 'ss' then 'ion' just needs to be added.
24 **division** The word given ends in 'de' so this is removed and 'sion' is added.
25 **invasion**   26 **explosion**
27 **rotation** The word given ends in 'te' so this is removed and 'tion' is added.
28 **collision**
29 **comprehension** 'Comprehend' ends in 'd' so this is removed and 'sion' is added.
30 **confession** The word ends in 'ss' so 'ion' just needs to be added.
31 **deflection** The word ends in 't' so this is removed and 'tion' is added.
32–37 Refer to Paper 2 Q16–23 on suffixes. Here are some possible answers:
32 *The dextrous surgeon completed another successful surgery.*
33 *People found the woman to be conceited because she talked about herself so much.*
34 *The team was exhilarated when they won the match.*
35 *It was his persistence that led him to find the rare book.*
36 *I will pursue my studies at university next year.*
37 *It is important to yield to oncoming traffic at the junction.*
38–43 Contractions are words that have been shortened and joined together. Apostrophes are added to show where letters have been removed from the words.
38 **we are**
39 **should have**
40 **I will**
41 **will not**
42 **let us**
43 **shall not**
44–49 Ensure each sentence used the listed phrase correctly. Note that the introduction of a hyphen into the phrase changes its meaning, e.g. *a hot water bottle – a water bottle that feels hot; a hot-water bottle – a container filled with hot water to warm a bed.*
44 *The equipment was very robust; it was a heavy metal detector.*
45 *He looked for mercury and cadmium with his heavy-metal detector.*
46 *She dropped the hot water bottle when it burned her hand.*
47 *He fell asleep holding his hot-water bottle.*
48 *Across the restaurant she saw a man eating crocodile steaks.*
49 *The man-eating crocodile prowled along the river bank.*
50–57 An antonym is a word that has the opposite meaning to the word given. Here are some possible answers:
50 *add, increase*
51 *whisper, mumble, murmur*
52 *contract, shrink, reduce*
53 *most, majority*
54 *participant, player, contributor*
55 *unconfident, hesitant, unsure*

56 *break, shatter*
57 *interior, inside*
58 **was** becomes **is** The Stamp family can't move until the removal truck is here.
59 **me** becomes **I** Kyle and I went swimming.
60 **is** becomes **are** Darren, Wusai and I are a good team.
61 **weren't** becomes **wasn't** The paint wasn't drying quickly enough.
62 **no** becomes **any** Najib didn't want any tea.
63 **migrate** The prefix 'trans' has been added.
64 **introduce** The prefix 're' has been added.
65 **section** The prefix 'inter' has been added.
66 **debate** 'r' has been added to create the suffix 'er'.
67 **consist** The suffix 'ent' has been added.
68 **resist** The suffix 'ance' has been added.
69 **freeze** The prefix 'anti' has been added.
70 **mighty** The prefix 'al' has been added.
71–82 'Quick!' called Laura. 'If we hurry we can catch the bus from Waterloo Road.'
83–89 'Come on then,' shouted Anna, as she raced off.
90–92 Refer to Paper 1 Q87–92 on clauses and Paper 1 Q83–86 on verbs. Here are some possible answers:
90 *I read a book each night that terrified me before I went to sleep.*
91 *My mum takes the bus to work but my dad rides his bicycle.*
92 *I ate my supper while I listened to the radio.*
93–100 In most cases when making a noun plural the letter 's' just needs to be added; or if the word ends in 's', 'ss', 'ff', 'sh', 'ch', 'x' or 'z' then 'es' is added. If a word ends in a single 'f', the 'f' is removed and 'ves' is added. However, there are exceptions to this rule (for example 'beliefs' and 'roofs') and these words need to be learned separately. If the word ends in 'y', this is removed and 'ies' is added. If a word ends in a vowel followed by an 'o', 's' just needs to be added.
93 **waltzes** As the word ends in 'z', 'es' needs to be added.
94 **glasses** As the word ends in 'ss', 'es' needs to be added.
95 **chiefs** This is an exception to the rule of words ending in 'f'; 's' just needs to be added.
96 **scenarios** As the word ends in a vowel followed by 'o', 's' just needs to be added.
97 **identities** As the word ends in 'y', this letter is removed and 'ies' is added.
98 **successes**
99 **werewolves** As the word ends in 'f', this letter is removed and 'ves' is added.
100 **quizzes**

Paper 4 (pages 20–26)

1 **because the bridge wasn't safe to cross** (line 7)
2 **snowy** (line 15)
3 **French** (line 53)
4 *the next place the train was to stop / a town / a train station* (line 3)
5 *The author uses this description to highlight to the reader that the bridge was originally built hastily and with little care, hence it is now unsafe to cross.*
6–8 insolent – *rude or disrespectful*
sage – *prudent, wise*
perceived – *believed, became aware of*
9 *that Passepartout tended to agree with the colonel*
10–11 *Many of the passengers declared openly that they felt the engineer's plan was a good one. The more people that believed it was a good idea and said so, the more others would be persuaded without possibly thinking through the consequences.*
12 *Towards the end of the passage the conductor cries 'All aboard!' (line 55).*
13 *an athlete / a long-jumper*
14–15 *Colonel Proctor can be described as an overbearing, dominating and loud person, e.g. Colonel Proctor is quite loud and enjoys being the centre of attention. This is shown when, after the engineer has made his proposal, the colonel begins to tell stories about trains leaping over rivers without bridges.* (lines 44–45)
16–24 The letters 'ei' are usually added after the letter 'c' and 'ie' is used after all other letters. However, there are exceptions to this rule (such as seize, neither, foreign, etc.) and these spellings needs to be learned separately.
16 **pierce**
17 **brief**
18 **conceive**
19 **feint**
20 **weigh**
21 **deceive**
22 **retrieve**
23 **freight**
24 **deceit**
25–29 A conjunction is a word that is used to join two main clauses together. It can also join a main clause to a subordinate clause. A subordinate clause is not a complete sentence, e.g. *'as the bus was late'*. Refer to Paper 1 Q87–92 on clauses. Examples of conjunctions are: *and, but, when, because,* etc. Possible answers:
25 *as / when*

EXPANDED ANSWERS

Bond English Assessment Papers 10–11+ years Book 2

A5

26 *while / as*
27 *until*
28 *because*
29 *but*
30–35 A metaphor is a direct comparison between two objects or actions. Whereas in a simile the words 'like' or 'as' are used, in a metaphor the words 'is', 'was', 'are', 'am', etc. are used. Here are some possible answers:
30 *The moon is a white balloon in the sky.*
31 *The dress is a shimmering sea of blue.*
32 *The fog was a blanket covering me.*
33 *The fireworks were a rainbow of colours in the sky.*
34 *The sleeping cat is a bundle of fluff beside the fire.*
35 *The crashing waves are a raging bull.*
36–50 'Tom, are you awake?' whispered Emily. 'I can't find the torch I've brought and I'm scared.'
51–57 Refer to Paper 2 Q16–23 on suffixes.
51 **neighbourhood**
52 **defenceless**
53 **friendship**
54 **kindness**
55 **scarceness**
56 **doubtless**
57 **spaceship**
58 **men's ward** As 'men' is a plural word, an apostrophe followed by an 's' ('s) is added.
59 **dog's ball** As the item only belongs to one thing, an apostrophe followed by an 's' ('s) is added.
60 **car's wheel**
61 **pony's stable**
62 **puppy's toy**
63–70 A compound word is a word made up of two separate words. For example, *tooth* and *brush* can be put together to form the word *toothbrush*.
weekend, nowhere, landmark, jackpot, printout, inlet, ongoing, goodwill
71 **past** The word 'fell' shows the action happened in the past.
72 **present** The words 'is covering' show the action is happening now.
73 **past** The word 'went' shows the action happened in the past.
74 **future** The auxiliary/helper verb will shows that the lesson will take place in the future.
75 **present** The word 'pecks' shows that the action is happening now.
76 **future** The auxiliary/helper verb 'will' shows that the fireworks will take place in the future.
77 **past** The word 'rained' shows the action happened in the past.
78–79 *less reliable, more reliable*

80–81 *less manageable, more manageable*
82–83 *less visible, more visible*
84–92 If a word has more than one syllable, one of the vowels is pronounced less forcefully and this is called an 'unstressed vowel'.
84 u s u (a) l l y
85 l i s t (e) n e r
86 b u s (i) n e s s
87 p e t (a) l
88 v a l u (a) b l e
89 t r a v (e) l l e r
90 c h o c (o) l a t e
91 d e s p (e) r a t e
92 h i s t (o) r y
93–97 (1) **important** (2) **imposition** (3) **impossible** (4) **impoverish** (5) **impracticable**
98–100 Bullet points are used to break down a list to make it easier to read. The list needs to be introduced with a colon (:) and each item needs a bullet point before it. Capital letters are not needed in a list of single words, but they are needed in a list of sentences. For example:
My favourite hobbies include:
• *painting*
• *cooking*
• *cycling*
Child's answer needs to show bullet points used within a paragraph.

Paper 5 (pages 27–32)

1 **two** (line 9)
2 **Norway** (line 10)
3 **Amundsen** (line 22)
4 *to move a thing using human effort*
5–6 *barren, deserted, dismal, challenging, cold, dangerous, etc.*
7–9 Acceptable answers could include any three of the following points: *Amundsen started closer to the Pole (line 27); he had a more experienced team (line 28); he laid more food depots (line 30); he concentrated on being first to the Pole and didn't collect samples and make observations on the way (lines 33–35).*
10 *Scott had to return before the winter with its freezing temperatures and constant darkness set in (lines 38–39).*
11–12 *Amundsen was an organised, skilled explorer who had courage and determination. His skill as an explorer is shown in the way he set out more, but smaller, food depots as he knew what to expect and what his team would need.*
13 *the date Scott set off on the expedition and the date he died (lines 5, 12–13)*
14 *from his journals (line 51–52)*

A6

15 *Oates realised he was going to die and wanted to do so away from the others hence stating 'I may be some time' but really knowing he would never return.*

16–22 Refer to Paper 4 Q84–92 on unstressed vowels.

16 **machinery**
17 **favourite**
18 **memory**
19 **jewellery**
20 **impatient**
21 **miserable**
22 **business**

23–33 To change the sentences from singular to plural, an 's' will need to be added to the noun. Make sure pronouns and verbs (such as 'was' or 'were') are also changed correctly.

23–26 The **girls were** riding **their horses**.
27–29 The **rabbits** fled down **their burrows**.
30–33 **They** saved **the stamps** to add to **their collections**.

34–36 An abbreviation is a word or group of words that have had letters removed. It may be formed from the first and last letter of a word, the first few letters of a word, or the intial letters of a group of words.

34 **Do it yourself**
35 **postage and packaging**
36 **Doctor**

37–44 A common noun is a person, place or thing. A proper noun is the name of a person, place or thing. A collective noun is a word describing a group. An abstract noun is a thought, feeling or idea.

common nouns	collective nouns	proper nouns	abstract nouns
grass	team	Harry	happiness
flame	gang	December	opinion

45–51 Possible answers:
45 **avoided**
46 **improving**
47 **repeatedly**
48 **inverted**
49 **Recently**
50 **return**
51 **pedestrian**

52–61 As Zoe and Rupa slept soundly strange things began to happen. A Night to Remember, the book Rupa had been reading, suddenly fell open at a page. The page told the story of a ghost which haunted the streets of Skegness every Thursday night.

62–69 Refer to Paper 2 Q16–23 on root words and suffixes. Possible answers:

62–63 *loving, lovely*
64–65 *clearly, cleared*
66–67 *cyclist, cycling*   **68–69** *payment, paying*

70–76 When the root word ends in a vowel, then the suffix 'cial' is used. When the root word ends in a consonant, 'tial' is used. The root words have been given below wherever possible.

70 **official** The root word is 'office' so 'cial' is added.
71 **financial** The root word is 'finance' so 'cial' is added.
72 **special** There is no root word for 'special', so this spelling needs to be learned separately.
73 **partial** The root word is 'part' so 'tial' is added.
74 **confidential** The root word is 'confident' so 'tial' is added.
75 **commercial** The root word is 'commerce' so 'cial' is added.
76 **essential** The root word is 'essence' and is an exception to the rule, so this spelling needs to be learned separately.

76–84 Refer to Paper 1 Q87–92 on clauses and Paper 4 Q25–29 on subordinate clauses.
76–78 <u>**Wes thought he was dreaming**</u> after he saw the flying squirrel.
79–80 <u>**My dad collapsed into his chair**</u> because the run had exhausted him!
81–82 <u>**Glass smashed everywhere**</u> when the picture fell from the wall.
83–84 <u>**Judy wondered whether she should read the book**</u> before she started her project.

85–88 A phrase is a small group of words, e.g. a cup of tea, to his left or his bicycle. A phrase cannot be a sentence on its own. Possible answers:
85 *in answer to your letter*
86 *you can get a form from*
87 *if you want to come*
88 *we are letting you know*

89–94 'Where is Jess?' moaned Dad. 'We really need to get going or we will miss our ferry.' / 'She is coming. I can hear her racing down the stairs,' replied Mum. / 'About time too!' continued Dad. / As Jess climbed into the car, Mum enquired, 'Have you got your coat?' / 'Oops … shall I go and get it?' Jess asked. / 'Yes and be VERY quick,' Dad almost shouted. 'I'm losing my patience!' / 'Sorry,' she called as she flew into the house.

95 (3)
96 (2)
97 (1)
98 (3)
99 (1)
100 (2)

1 **Ireland** (line 2)
2 **Pat** (line 8)
3 **winter** (line 19)
4–5 *because she had died or because she had asked him to leave*
6–7 *The poem implies that his only friend and companion is Tray: 'I had always a friend in my poor dog Tray' (line 12). His sense of loss is evident when Tray dies*
8 *He had no (or very little) money in his wallet.*
9–11 *Tray provided companionship, he provided warmth at night and he guided Pat, as Pat was blind. This is shown in the lines 'Where now shall I go, poor, forsaken, and blind? Can I find one to guide me, so faithful and kind?' (lines 21–22).*
12–14 *The poem begins with a contented man with a loving relationship and a dog but when separated from Sheelah he found himself poor and homeless. He accepted his fate and didn't fight it though he felt lonely but for his dog. After Tray died he felt even more isolated and vulnerable.*
15 Child's opinion on whom, after reading the poem, they feel sorrier for, the dog or the man, with an explanation for their answer, e.g. *I feel sorrier for the man because he is now left on his own and must try to survive.*
16–20 Refer to Paper 5 Q37–44 on nouns and questions Paper 1 Q83–86 on verbs. Nouns can be changed into verbs by adding a suffix; in this case 'ment', 'or' and 'ion'. The suffix 'ment' just needs to be added. The 'or' suffix usually follows the letters 'ct', 'it', 'at', 'rr' or 'ess'. Refer to Paper 3 Q24–31 on adding the 'ion' suffix. However, if a word ends in in 'ne', 've', 'le', 'se' or 're', the 'e' needs to be removed and replaced with 'ation'.
16 **rejection**
17 **compilation**
18 **government**
19 **auditor**
20 **confession**
21–28 Refer to Paper 3 Q50–57 on antonyms and Paper 2 Q93–100 on prefixes. The prefix 'im' is added to words beginning with 'm' or 'p'; 'ir' is added to words beginning with 'r'; and 'il' is added to words beginning with 'l'. Other words will need the correct prefix chosen from the following: 'un', 'dis' or 'in'.
21 **unimportant**
22 **irresistible**
23 **disregard**
24 **immature**
25 **inconsistent**
26 **illogical**
27 **disown**
28 **impatient**
29–32 Refer to Paper 1 Q52–54 on double negatives.
29 **Jake didn't borrow a book from the library.**
30 **Gina said she wasn't playing her music too loud.** 'The music' can be used instead of 'her music'.
31 **There isn't a football match this weekend.** 'Is no' can be used instead of 'isn't a'.
32 **There wasn't time to have dinner before going to the cinema.** 'Was no' can be used instead of 'wasn't'.
33 ex**h**ibition
34 s**c**issors
35 solem**n**
36 g**u**itar
37 **m**nemonic
38 cu**p**board
39 dum**b**struck
40 whis**t**le
41–48 'What time is it, Miss Morris?' queried Kyle.
49–54 Finn screamed, 'Watch out!'
55–65 'Don't stand there, there's broken glass,' said Tracey. 'You might cut yourself.'
66–69 Refer to Paper 2 Q43–48 on proverbs.
66 **right**
67 **worm**
68 **lives**
69 **nine**
70–71 A fronted adverbial is a word or phrase that has been moved to the beginning of a sentence and is usually followed by a comma. For example, the sentence *'She read her book later that morning.'* can be rearranged with a fronted adverbial: *'Later that morning, she read her book.'* Other examples of fronted adverbials are: *All of a sudden, Usually, Nearby, Frequently.* Child's answer needs to be two sentences, each starting with a fronted adverbial. Possible answers:
72 *You will be notified shortly.*
73 *A form can be obtained from the office.*
74 *Keep off the grass.*
75 *We will inform you of our decision.*
76–80 A preposition is a word that tells us how one thing relates to another. Prepositions tell us the position, direction or time of something.
76 **on**
77 **under**
78 **in**
79 **through**
80 **underneath**

81–86 Words in the past tense tell us about things that have already happened. The correct verb form will need to be used (refer to Paper 1 Q83–86 on verbs). Usually the letters 'ed' just need to be added to make the past tense. However, there are irregular verbs which will need to be spelled differently (e.g. *grew, crept, drank,* etc). Words such as 'was', 'had' and 'did' are also verbs, as they show a 'state of being'. Here are some possible answers:

81 *ran*
82 *broke*
83 *ate*
84 *was*
85 *poured*
86 *were*

87–92 When the 'fer' sound in the word is pronounced more forcefully after a suffix is added, the 'r' needs to be doubled. If it is not pronounced more forcefully, it remains a single 'r'.

87 **referral** The emphasis is on the 'fer' sound, so 'r' is doubled and the suffix is added.
88 **referring**
89 **preferring**
90 **preference** The emphasis is on the 'pre' and 'ence' sound, so the 'r' is not doubled.
91 **transferred** *Ref*
92 **transferring**.

93–100 Refer to Paper 2 Q16–23 on suffixes.

93 **justifiable** The word ends in a consonant followed by a 'y', so the 'y' is changed to 'i' and the suffix is added.
94 **earliest**
95 **employment** The word ends in a vowel followed by a 'y', so the suffix just needs to be added.
96 **ladyship** This is an exception to the rule of words ending in 'y' and the suffix just needs to be added.
97 **hungrily**
98 **beautiful**
99 **occupied**
100 **studious**

Paper 7 (pages 38–44)

1 **on his own** (line 3)
2 **because the demand for their release was too strong** (line 21)
3 **winter** (line 31)
4 *because he thought Robben Island was a prison with freedoms and because it is an island it would have sea views*
5–6 *Lieutenant Van Wyck's speech cheered Nelson Mandela as it gave him strength to believe that*

he might leave prison relatively soon and that the cause he fought for was worthwhile and had the backing of many – otherwise release would not be considered.

7 **30 years** (line 25)
8 *As Nelson Mandela had many supporters it was easier for the police to move him without them knowing and under the cover of darkness. Otherwise it might stir up more problems for the police to deal with.*
9 *mysteriously*
10 *noisy, energetic, excited*
11 Yes: 'the atmosphere was tense but quiet, unlike the boisterous reception I had received on my arrival on the island two years before.' (lines 32–33)
12 *He didn't intend to be treated as a boy when he was a man and in the winter it was unreasonable to expect anyone to wear shorts.* (lines 41–42)
13–15 *Despite the strength Nelson Mandela obviously found in the cause he was imprisoned for he must have felt tired, depressed and cold. The living conditions were so poor and the unknown must have been daunting. This is shown when he describes how he could walk the length of his cell in three paces* (line 45), *which shows how small and cramped a space he was forced to live in.*
16–24 When adding these suffixes, it helps to say the words aloud. The suffix 'ant' is used if there is a related word with an '-ation' ending, e.g. hesitation – hesitant, hesitancy. The 'ent' suffix is also used after a 'soft c' and 'soft g' sound (refer to Paper 2 Q56–63 on soft c and g). However, there are exceptions to this rule and these words need to be learned separately.

16 **reluctant**
17 **irrelevant**
18 **recipient**
19 **imminent**
20 **consistent**
21 **important**
22 **valiant**
23 **inefficient**
24 **extravagant**
25–28 Indirect speech tells us about what someone has said and does not use inverted commas. In indirect speech, phrases such as 'said that' and 'shouted to' are used. In addition, the tense of the verb may sometimes change, for example from present to past.

25 **The teacher informed Jake's mum that he had hurt himself at school today.**
26 **Lena giggled excitedly that it looked like it might snow.**

27 **Rory enquired what time the match was.**

28 **Sam informed her class that the police were investigating her missing bike.**

29–33 Child's own passage debating the subject of recycling at his/her school. The following words need to be included: *evidence, furthermore, conclusion, summary, predict,* e.g. *There is a great deal of scientific evidence that shows the benefits of recycling. I have investigated the amount of recycling done at our school and have reached the conclusion that much more can be done to recycle and help the environment. Furthermore, by recycling we are showing the community that we students care about what happens outside our school walls. In summary, I predict that if we begin to recycle cans and glass, we can reduce the amount of rubbish we put in landfills by 50 per cent.*

34–40 Refer to Paper 5 Q34–36 on abbreviations.

34 **New Zealand**

35 **approximately**

36 **Heavy Goods Vehicle**

37 **millimetre**

38 **very important person**

39 **television**

40 **rest in peace**

41–45 Refer to Paper 1 Q23–31 and 55–56 on commas and parentheses.

41–43 *My school backpack is so heavy because I have to carry my books, lunch box, PE kit, pencil case and ring binder.*

44–45 *My sister, who is ten years old, is acting in a pantomime this week.*

46–52 Refer to Paper 5 Q–44 on nouns; Paper 1 Q40–46 on adverbs; Paper 1 Q83–86 on verbs; Paper 4 Q25–29 on conjunctions; and Paper 2 Q31–36 on adjectives. A pronoun a word that replaces a noun in a sentence to avoid repetition, e.g. *I, she, they, it* and *we.*

46 **hate**

47 **faintly**

48 **scatter**

49 **litter**

50 **because**

51 **masterful**

52 **it**

53–59 Refer to Paper 1 Q83–86 on active and passive verbs.

53 **active**

54 **active**

55 **active**

56 **passive**

57 **active**

58 **active**

59 **passive**

60 **relevant**

61 **conscience**

62 **mischievous**

63 **beginning**

64 **completely**

65 **hindrance**

66 **convenience**

67 **unnecessary**

68–72 Refer to Paper 1 Q87–92 on clauses and Paper 4 Q25–29 on subordinate clauses and conjunctions. Here are some possible answers:

68 *The horse galloped across the field because the farmer was chasing it.*

69 *The waiter tripped holding two plates of food and it went all over the floor!*

70 *The baby slept peacefully while his mother watched over him.*

71 *Poppy finally finished her book and she took it back to the library.*

72 *At last the audience were seated after they had applauded enthusiastically.*

73–77 Refer to Paper 2 Q87–90 on similes.

73 **mouse**

74 **ox**

75 **dust / a bone**

76 **ice**

77 **fiddle**

78–95 'What are you doing looking in my bag?' I asked.
'Is it yours?' Ben sneered. 'I was wondering what my MP3 player was doing in it.'
I stared in disbelief.

96–100 Refer to Paper 4 Q84–92 on unstressed vowels.

96 e n t r **a** n c e

97 d i c t i o n **a** r y

98 f r i g h t **e** n i n g

99 h i s t **o** r y

100 d i e s **e** l

Paper 8 (pages 44–49)

1 **orange and guava juice** (lines 4–5)

2 **follow his daughter** (lines 45–46)

3 **leg** (line 12)

4 *because different cultures allow their children to grow up with different freedoms; obviously this school has a range of children from different cultures (lines 19–20) so Mr Patel's daughter is bound to embrace these outside the confines of home*

5–6 insolent – *behaving in an insulting way* imperceptibly – *undetectably*

7 *he felt they couldn't be trusted*

8–9 *Mma Ramotswe did not agree with Mr Patel*

A10

that children should be watched. This is shown when she says, 'Although I must say I don't really like doing this. I don't like the idea of watching a child.' (lines 33–34)

10 *He was becoming upset that his daughter would not tell him the name of the boy.*

11 *because she wanted to keep her anonymity, otherwise following her would be very hard (lines 50–51)*

12–13 *Mma Ramotswe and Mr Patel had little in common. Mma Ramotswe couldn't understand his desire to control his daughter to the extent he wanted to, she felt he hadn't caught up with modern-day living and the freedoms this allowed (lines 39–41). She also wasn't too keen on his attitudes towards women (lines 52–53). This is shown when she says that she is a modern woman who has different ideas from him (line 43).*

14 *In his view being a detective was a man's job, not a woman's.*

15 *to show that Mma Ramotswe believes that it is important for parents to be able to let their children go*

16–27 '(H)ow long until we get to (U)ncle (R)on's house?' groaned (S)imon.
'(N)ot long now. (T)ake a left down (T)iffany (S)treet and then we are there,' answered his dad.
(T)hey had been cycling for the last two hours and the novelty of the ride had begun to wear off. (T)he newspaper article '(G)etting (F)it' had been right, maybe it would be better to do it in short manageable cycle rides!

28–34 Refer to Paper 4 Q63–70 on compound words.
tablecloth, database, schoolteacher, uttermost, checkout, redhead, well-being

35–40 Refer to Paper 4 Q25–29 on conjunctions. Possible answers.

35 *until*

36 *as*

37 *although*

38 *because / when*

39 *but*

40 *if*

41 **atlas** As the root word ends in an 's', 'es' has been added so this just needs to be removed.

42 **syllabus** A plural word that ends in 'i' has been adapted from a word ending in 'us'; the 'i' needs to be removed and replaced with 'us'.

43 **emergency** A plural word ending in 'ies' has been adapted from a word ending in 'y'; 'ies' needs to be removed and replaced with 'y'.

44 **runway** This word just needs the 's' removed.

45 **speech** As the root word ends in an 'ch', 'es' has been added so this just needs to be removed.

46 **larva** A plural word ending in 'ae' has been adapted from a word ending in 'a'; the 'e' just needs to be removed.

47–50 Refer to Paper 1 Q87–92 and Paper 4 Q25–29 on clauses and Paper 5 Q85–88 on phrases. Here are some possible answers:

47 *It took several minutes before they realised where they were and what they had to do now.*

48 *The thought of it terrified the giant so he ran away as fast as he could!*

49 *The bird crashed into the closed window, cracking the glass.*

50 *The teacher's explanation confused Kelly even more so she asked again.*

51–57 Refer to Paper 1 Q16–22 on synonyms. Here are some possible answers: *kind, beautiful, pleasant, exquisite, attractive, friendly, delicious*

58 There **was** time to get home before our friends arrived.

59 Marianne **is** comfortable in her bed.

60 The dogs **were** chasing after the rabbit.

61 There **is** a knock at the door.

62 Tim and Sally **are** best friends.

63–69 'Goodbye,' called the zoo keeper. 'Don't come back next time a lion escapes!' / 'Wow!' smiled Meena. 'I didn't think we were going to get out alive!' / 'Me neither,' said Rudi. / 'What was the scariest moment, Rudi?' / 'When you slipped over as the lion started running towards us!' giggled Rudi. / 'Mine too!' / 'Let's go home and tell your mum.' / 'She'll never believe us!'

70–75 Refer to Paper 4 Q30–35 on metaphors. Here are some possible answers:

70 *The clouds were cotton balls.*

71 *The snow was a white blanket.*

72 *The waterfall was a snake, slowly sliding down the mountain.*

73 *The bull was a tank coming towards me!*

74 *The dew is a glittering carpet.*

75 *The quilt was a rainbow of colours.*

76-83 Possible answers:

76 *fought, caught*

77 *bough, cow*

78 *tough, fluff*

79 *thought, taught*

80 *dough, blow*

81 *borough*

82–83 *cough, through*

84–93 'Two' means the number two; 'to' tells us the direction or position of something or the relationship of one thing to another, or it can be part of the infinitive form of a verb; 'too' means 'as well' or 'overly'.

84–86 **to**, **two**, **to** It is time to take the two dogs for a walk to the park.

87–88 **too**, **to** He's not too well today so I'm taking him to the doctor's.

89–90 **to**, **two** I think we should start to cook the two fish on the BBQ.

91–93 **too**, **two**, **to** I'll have to undo two trouser buttons to feel comfortable because I've eaten too much.

94–100 Refer to Paper 2 Q93–100 on prefixes.

  94 *precaution*
  95 *misconstrue*
  96 *confront, affront*
  97 *reconnect, disconnect, interconnect*
  98 *expatriate, repatriate*
  99 *co-education*
  100 *abnormal, paranormal, subnormal*

Paper 9 (pages 50–56)

1 **to raise funds for leukaemia research** (lines 6–7)

2 **Michael/David/Tam** (line 28)

3 **its theme park** (lines 37–38)

4 *With her family arriving she felt she had finished her journey and Dan was the only one missing and she wanted him to be part of it.*

5 *when everything freezes; when you are aware of everything around you*

6 *Time stood still for Sally because seeing her family again at the end of her walk was a time of great happiness and emotion.*

7 *She felt elated and carefree as she set out on the final day of walking with her family around her – nothing worried her. She now knew for sure she would achieve her goal.*

8–9 **lull** (line 17) and **scrutinising** (line 34)

10–12 *Evidence supporting how Sally felt on completing her walk; happy, content, overwhelmed, tired, excited, etc. 'Sally felt excited and happy for completing her walk. This is shown when she says that everyone looked wonderful and that it was an extraordinary day.'*

13–15 Characteristics of Sally's personality that helped her achieve her goal, e.g. *brave, determined, strong.* Child needs to give reasons, e.g. *Sally is a brave and caring person. She is brave because she undertook a difficult challenge that lasted many months and which she did on her own. She is caring because she did the walk to raise money for leukaemia research even though her son had died.*

16–20 Refer to Paper 5 Q37–44 on nouns. The infinitive of a verb is the most basic form of the word and is preceded by the word 'to', e.g. *to talk* is the infinitive of *talking* or *talked.*

16 **to advertise**
17 **to depart**
18 **to fly**
19 **to applaud**
20 **to conclude**
21 **the girls' hats** As the items belong to more than one person or thing, an 's' followed by an apostrophe (s') is added.
22 **the churches' spires**
23 **Lilia's home** As the item only belongs to one person or thing, an apostrophe followed by an 's' ('s) is added.
24 **James's computer** or **James' computer** As this is a singular noun that already ends in an 's', an apostrophe followed by an 's' ('s) or an apostrophe at the end of the word is acceptable.
25 **his friend's bike**.
26 **the teacher's scissors**
27–38 Refer to Paper 1 Q83–86 on verbs and 31–36 on adjectives. Here are some possible answers:
27–30 *The **cautious** girl **moved** carefully towards the gate as the **frightened** horse was **galloping** across the field.*
31–34 *The **colourful** kite **was dancing** in the **blue** sky as a **gentle** wind **blew**.*
35–38 *Monty, the **playful** dog, **pounced** on his **favourite** ball, then **gave** it to the man.*
39 *without furniture*
40 *in low spirits*
41 *polite*
42 *a person who watches*
43 *helped*
44 *attempt (noun) or to try (verb)*
45 *to look like*
46–53 Refer to Paper 1 Q57–65 on homophones
46 **practice**
47 **practise**
48 **principal**
49 **principle**
50 **their**
51 **there**
52 **course**
53 **coarse**
54 **omelette**
55 **minnow**
56 **shallow**
57 **flannel**
58 **arrive**
59 **quarrel**
60 **goggle**
61 **struggle**
62–67 A colon (:) is used to introduce a list, explanation or quotation, e.g. *I visited the following places last year: Cornwall, Scotland*

A12

and Wales. A semi-colon (;) is used in place of a conjunction (e.g. *but, and, etc*) to join two sentences together, e.g. *She felt happy; it was her birthday*. It is also used in place of commas in complex lists, e.g. *She received many presents: a set of watercolour paints; a book by her favourite author; and a beautiful new dress*. It is worth noting that a semi-colon is placed before the conjunction 'and' at the end of a list.

62 **It's snowing; I'm so excited.**

63–66 **People enjoy summer for a number of reasons: it's warm; they enjoy doing things outside; they can have BBQs; it stays light late into the evening.**

67 **We have two types of tree in our garden: beech and oak.**

68 **lump of lead – head**

69 **skin and blister – sister**

70 **frog and toad – road**

71 **mince pies – eyes**

72 **sugar and honey – money**

73 **dog and bone – telephone**

74 **Barnet Fair – hair**

75–79 Helper verbs are sometimes known as auxiliary verbs. They are used with a main verb to show which tense the sentence is in. Examples of helper verbs are: am, are, were, will, be, can, etc. Here are some possible answers:

75 *shall, might, will, may*

76 *will, might, can*

77 *won't, shan't*

78 *would, should*

79 *will, might, may*

80–86 Refer to Paper 1 Q16–22 on synonyms. Possible answers:

80 **annually**

81 **frequently**

82 **regretted**

83 **decided**

84 **audience**

85 **congregation**

86 **Occasionally**

87–94 A superlative is an adjective or adverb that expresses the highest quality of something, e.g. *tallest, fastest, happiest*. Most words just need the suffix 'est' added; however, some words change completely, e.g. *best*, or need to be preceded by the word 'most', e.g. *most beautiful, most famous*.

87 **cleverest**

88 **poorest**

89 **worst**

90 **ugliest**

91 **reddest**

92 **most generous**

93 **best**

94 **most curious**

95–100 A diminutive is a word that describes a smaller version of something.

owlet, duckling, piglet, lambkin, statuette, eaglet

Paper 10 (pages 57–62)

1 **cleaning the silver** (line 22)

2 **bullets** (line 30)

3–6 *The story is about a town that is bombed during a war. This is shown by the all-clear siren (line 4), the flattened machine-gun bullets (lines 30–31) and the fact that road surface has been damaged by bullets (lines 37–38).*

7 *because she was shocked by the damage done to the room*

8 *'knives and forks like a shoal of shining fish.' (lines 13–14)*

9 *dotted with small holes*

10 *She reacted in this way because she was probably dazed, confused and worried about what had happened.*

11 *'Then she realised that whatever had done it had passed straight through the spot where she had been standing cleaning the silver.' (lines 21–22)*

12 *'Staring at the tea-roses peeping over Mr Marshall's fence, the same as they did every year.' (lines 45–46)*

13–15 *At first she is confused about what has happened and focuses entirely on her immediate surroundings. She then becomes worried about the safety of others, as is shown when she runs outside to check on the milkman. The enormity of what has happened hits her making her feel very weary (line 44) and yet only when someone shows concern for her does she feel her emotions might take hold, as when she says she nearly wept, but she keeps herself in check (line 50).*

16–23 Refer to Paper 2 Q16–23 on root words.

16 **sign** The suffix 'ature' has been added.

17 **hope** The suffixes 'ful' and 'ly' have been added.

18 **state** The suffix 'ment' has been added.

19 **doubt** The suffix 'ful' has been added.

20 **decorate** The 'e' has been removed and the suffix 'tion' has been added.

21 **lazy** The 'y' has been changed to an 'i' and the suffix 'ly' has been added.

22 **instant** The suffix 'aneous' has been added.

23 **extend** The 'd' has been removed and the suffix 'sion' has been added.

24–25 Apostrophes are used to show who or what something belongs to. When it belongs to one person or thing, the word ends in an apostrophe followed by an 's' ('s), e.g. *The boy's toy.* When it belongs to more than one, then 's' is added followed by an apostrophe (s'), e.g. *the ladies' shoes.* When words have been shortened, apostrophes are added to show where letters have been removed, e.g. *I'm, didn't, can't, isn't.* These are also referred to as contractions.

24–25 I'm sorry we're going to be late.
26 Liz fed Aimee's ducks.
27 Where's the party?
28 The dogs' coats were muddy and wet.
29–31 Let's hide Jake's homework here, he'll never find it.
32–38 Refer to Paper 6 Q76–80 on prepositions. Possible answers:
32 *between*
33 *behind*
34 *on*
35 *into*
36 *in, around*
37 *between*
38 *into*
39 baroness
40 niece
41 nanny-goat
42 duck
43 duchess
44 doe or **hind**
45–48 An noun phrase is a small group of words that describe a noun e.g. *coated with chocolate, dazzlingly white, very beautiful, etc.* Here are some possible examples:
45 *a horse covered with medals*
46 *the radiant, gleaming moon*
47 *a very frightening film*
48 *the fierce, blustery wind*
49 autum**n**

50 ki**t**chen
51 han**d**kerchief
52 su**b**tlety
53 **p**salm
54 s**c**ience
55 **w**rench
56 colum**n**
57 insistent
58 insinuate
59 insincere
60 inseparable
61 insensitive
62 inscription
64–89 'Who is there?' cried Steven, putting his head out of his bedroom window.
'It's Mike, Steven.'
'What do you want?' he asked.
'Sadie has fallen from the swings. Can you ask your dad to come as quickly as possible? She needs a doctor to check her leg.'
90–94 Refer to Paper 1 Q23–31 and 55–56 on commas and parentheses.
90–91 Every afternoon, as they were coming home from school, Mina and Toby used to play by the banks of the river.
92 It was a lovely large garden, with soft green grass. / It was a lovely, large garden with soft, green grass.
93–94 High above the city, on a tall column, stood the statue of Nelson.
95–96 A hyphen is a small dash that is inserted to help make a word's meaning clear. For example: recover and re-cover have two different meanings. Hyphens are also inserted between a prefix ending in a vowel and a root word beginning in a vowel. For example, co-own needs a hyphen as coown will not make sense.
95–96 *off-centre, off-colour, off-limits*
97–98 *non-stop, non-fiction*
99–100 *re-cover, re-elect*

A14

NOTES

NOTES

Write one word instead of the words in bold.

D 1

45 We **kept out of the way of** Mum because she was cross. _____

46 Mr Martin says that my work is **getting much better**. _____

47 In case we forgot, we said the message **over and over again**. _____

48 The fraction had to be **turned upside down**. _____

49 **A short time ago** we went to the circus. _____

50 The boy was told to **come back** tomorrow. _____

51 The cyclist knocked over a **person who was walking**. _____ **7**

Rewrite the following passage, adding the missing capital letters.

D 5

52–61 as zoe and rupa slept soundly strange things began to happen. a night to remember, the book rupa had been reading, suddenly fell open at a page. the page told the story of a ghost which haunted the streets of skegness every thursday night.

_____

_____

_____

_____ **10**

Add two more words that are based on the following **root words**.

D 11

Example: help   *helping*   *helpful*

62–63 love   _____   _____

64–65 clear   _____   _____

66–67 cycle   _____   _____

68–69 pay   _____   _____ **8**

Complete these words with *cial* or *tial*.

E 1

70 offi_____   71 finan_____

72 spe_____   73 par_____

74 confiden_____   75 commer_____

76 essen_____   **7**

Underline separately the **clauses** in each sentence.

77–78 Wes thought he was dreaming after he saw the flying squirrel.

79–80 My Dad collapsed into his chair because the run had exhausted him!

81–82 Glass smashed everywhere when the picture fell from the wall.

83–84 Judy wondered whether she should read the book before she started her project.

These **phrases** are often used in formal letters or documents. What do they mean?

85 further to your recent correspondence

_____

86 forms may be obtained from

_____

87 those wishing to attend

_____

88 notice is hereby served

_____

Draw a line (/) every time a new line should have been started in the following dialogue.

D 12

89–94 'Where is Jess?' moaned Dad. 'We really need to get going or we will miss our ferry.' 'She is coming, I can hear her racing down the stairs,' replied Mum. 'About time too!' continued Dad. As Jess climbed into the car, Mum enquired, 'Have you got your coat?' 'Oops ... shall I go and get it?' Jess asked. 'Yes and be VERY quick,' Dad almost shouted. 'I'm losing my patience!' 'Sorry,' she called as she flew into the house.

6

Write the number (1, 2 or 3) next to each word derived from:

    (1)   another language

    (2)   names of places or people

    (3)   imitating sounds

95 sizzle _____   **96** wellington _____

97 spaghetti _____   **98** splutter _____

99 photograph _____   **100** hoover _____

6

Now go to the Progress Chart to record your score!   **Total**   100

32

Poor Dog Tray

On the green banks of Shannon when Sheelah was nigh,
No blithe Irish lad was so happy as I;
No harp like my own could so cheerily play,
And wherever I went was my poor dog Tray.

When at last I was forced from my Sheelah to part,   5
She said (while the sorrow was big at her heart),
Oh! remember your Sheelah when far, far away:
And be kind, my dear Pat, to our poor dog Tray.

Poor dog! he was faithful and kind to be sure,
And he constantly loved me although I was poor;   10
When the sour-looking folk sent me heartless away,
I had always a friend in my poor dog Tray.

When the road was so dark, and the night was so cold,
And Pat and his dog were grown weary and old,
How snugly we slept in my old coat of grey,   15
And he lick'd me for kindness – my old dog Tray.

Though my wallet was scant I remember'd his case,
Nor refused my last crust to his pitiful face;
But he died at my feet on a cold winter day,
And I play'd a sad lament for my poor dog Tray.   20

Where now shall I go, poor, forsaken, and blind?
Can I find one to guide me, so faithful and kind?
To my sweet native village, so far, far away,
I can never more return with my poor dog Tray.

                                                        Thomas Campbell

Underline the correct answers.

  1 In which country is this poem set?

   (England, Ireland, Wales)

  2 What is the gentleman's name?

   (Sheelah, Tray, Pat)

  3 At what time of year did Tray die?

   (winter, summer, autumn)

Answer these questions.

4–5 Write two possible reasons why the man had to leave Sheelah.

_____

_____

6–7 Use evidence from the poem to explain how we know the man was lonely.

_____

_____

8 What is meant by 'Though my wallet was scant …' (line 17)?

_____

9–11 Give two reasons why the dog Tray is so important to the man. Use evidence from the passage to support your answer.

_____

_____

_____

12–14 Describe the personal journey this man makes through the poem. How does his self-worth change?

_____

_____

_____

15 Who in this poem do you feel more sorry for, the dog or the man? Why?

_____

12

D 6

Form **nouns** from the **verbs** in bold to fill each gap.

16 reject Bola had a sense of _____ as his dog ran off to meet his sister.

17 compile Brian put together a _____ of his favourite music.

18 govern The _____ insisted seat belts should be worn.

19 audit The _____ checked through the files thoroughly.

20 confess The burglar gave a detailed _____.

5

Write an **antonym** for each of these words by adding a **prefix**.

D 9
E 2

21 important _____ 22 resistible _____

23 regard _____ 24 mature _____

25 consistent _____ 26 logical _____

27 own _____ 28 patient _____

8

D 13

Rewrite these sentences without double negatives.

29 Jake didn't borrow no book from the library.

_____

30 Gina said she wasn't playing no music too loud.

_____

31 There isn't no football match this weekend.

_____

32 There wasn't no time to have dinner before going to the cinema.

_____

4

Rewrite each word, adding the missing silent letter so that each word is spelt correctly.

E 2

33 exibition _____ 34 sissors _____

35 solem _____ 36 gitar _____

37 nemonic _____ 38 cuboard _____

39 dumstruck _____ 40 whisle _____

8

Punctuate these sentences correctly.

D 5

41–48 what time is it miss morris queried kyle

_____

49–54 finn screamed watch out

_____

55–65 don't stand there there's broken glass said tracey you might cut yourself

_____

25

Complete the following proverbs.

C 4

66 Two wrongs don't make a _____.

67 The early bird catches the _____.

68 A fool and his _____ are soon parted.

69 A cat has nine _____.

4

Write two sentences that begin with a **fronted adverbial**.

D 6

70 _____

71 _____

2

Using official-type language, rewrite each of these sentences.

D 1

72 We will let you know soon.

_____

73 You can get a form from the office.

_____

74 Please don't walk on the grass.

_____

75 We will let you know what we decide.

_____

4

Underline the **prepositions** in the following sentences.

D 6

76 Ahmed slipped on the banana skin.

77 The hedgehog slept under the autumn leaves.

78 The test papers were hidden in amongst the workbooks.

79 The ball went through the goalie's legs!

80 Sam hid underneath his bed.

5

Complete each of these sentences in the **past tense**.

D 13

81 I _____ to school because I was late.

82 When I jumped off the wall I _____ my leg.

83 George _____ his lunch quickly.

84 Tess _____ late for the party.

85 It _____ with rain all day.

86 The children _____ playing on the climbing equipment.

⬤ 6

Complete these word sums.

87 refer + al = _____

88 refer + ing = _____

89 prefer + ing = _____

90 prefer + ence = _____

91 transfer + ed = _____

92 transfer + ing = _____

⬤ 6

Add the **suffixes** to these words ending in *y*. Don't forget any necessary spelling changes.

E 2

93 justify + able _____

94 early + est _____

95 employ + ment _____

96 lady + ship _____

97 hungry + ly _____

98 beauty + ful _____

99 occupy + ed _____

100 study + ous _____

⬤ 8

Now go to the Progress Chart to record your score!   Total ⬤ 100

Nelson Mandela was sentenced to life imprisonment and started his prison years in the notorious Robben Island Prison.

At midnight, I was awake and staring at the ceiling – images from the trial were still rattling around in my head – when I heard steps coming down the hallway. I was locked in my own cell, away from the others. There was a knock at my door and I could see Colonel Aucamp's face at the bars. 'Mandela,' he said in a husky whisper, 'are you awake?' 5

I told him I was. 'You are a lucky man,' he said. 'We are taking you to a place where you will have your freedom. You will be able to move around; you'll see the ocean and the sky, not just grey walls.'

He intended no sarcasm, but I well knew that the place he was referring to would not afford me the freedom I longed for. He then remarked rather cryptically, 'As long 10 as you don't make trouble, you'll get everything you want.'

Aucamp then woke the others, all of whom were in a single cell, ordering them to pack their things. Fifteen minutes later we were making our way through the iron labyrinth of Pretoria Local, with its endless series of clanging metal doors echoing in our ears. 15

Once outside, the seven of us – Walter, Raymond, Govan, Kathy, Andrew, Elias and myself – were handcuffed and piled into the back of a police van ... The warders provided us with sandwiches and cold drinks and Lieutenant Van Wyck was perched in the back with us. He was a pleasant fellow, and during a lull in the singing, he offered his unsolicited opinion on our future. 'Well,' he said, 'you chaps won't 20 be in prison long. The demand for your release is too strong. In a year or two, you will get out and you will return as national heroes. Crowds will cheer you, everyone will want to be your friend, women will want you. Ag, you fellows have it made.' We listened without comment, but I confess his speech cheered me considerably. Unfortunately, his prediction turned out to be off by nearly three decades. 25

We were departing quietly, secretly, under a heavy police escort, in the middle of the night, and in less than half an hour we found ourselves at a small military airport outside the city ...

From here Nelson was put on a plane to Robben Island.

... We landed on a military airstrip on one end of the island. It was a grim, overcast 30 day ... the cold winter wind whipped through our thin prison uniforms. We were met by guards with automatic weapons; the atmosphere was tense but quiet, unlike the boisterous reception I had received on my arrival on the island two years before.

We were driven to the old jail, an isolated stone building, where we were ordered to strip while standing outside. One of the ritual indignities of prison life is that 35 when you are transferred from one prison to another, the first thing that happens is that you change from the garb of the old prison to that of the new. When we were undressed, we were thrown the plain khaki uniforms of Robben Island.

Apartheid's regulations extended even to clothing. All of us, except Kathy, received short trousers, an insubstantial jersey, and a canvas jacket. Kathy, the one Indian   40
among us, was given long trousers ... Short trousers for Africans were meant to remind us that we were 'boys'. I put on the short trousers that day, but I vowed that I would not put up with them for long.

I was assigned a cell at the head of the corridor. It overlooked the courtyard and had a small eye-level window. I could walk the length of my cell in three paces.   45
When I lay down, I could feel the wall with my feet and my head grazed the concrete at the other side. The width was about six feet, and the walls were at least two feet thick. Each cell had a white card posted outside of it with our name and our prison service number. Mine read, 'N Mandela 466/64,' which meant I was the 466th prisoner admitted to the island in 1964. I was forty-six years old, a political   50
prisoner with a life sentence, and that small cramped space was to be my home for I knew not how long.

From *Long Walk to Freedom: The Autobiography of Nelson Mandela*

Underline the correct answers.

1   After the trial was Nelson Mandela in a cell on his own or with others?

(on his own, with others, the passage doesn't state)

2   Why did Lieutenant Van Wyck believe Nelson Mandela and his friends would soon be released?

(because they had served their sentence, because the demand for their release was too strong, because there wasn't room in the prison to detain them)

3   In which season did Nelson Mandela arrive at Robben Island?

(winter, spring, autumn)

3

Answer these questions.

4   Colonel Aucamp told Nelson Mandela he was a 'lucky' man (line 6). Why did he think Nelson Mandela was lucky?

_____

5–6   Give two reasons why you think Lieutenant Van Wyck's speech cheered Nelson Mandela.

_____

_____

7   For approximately how many years was Nelson Mandela in prison?

_____

8   Why do you think Nelson Mandela and his friends were 'departing quietly, secretly, under a heavy police escort, in the middle of the night' (line 26)?

_____

9 What does the word 'cryptically' mean (line 10)?

_____

10 What does the word 'boisterous' mean (line 33)?

_____

11 Had Nelson Mandela previously been to Robben Island? Copy the line from the passage that answers this question.

_____

12 Why do you think Nelson Mandela vowed that he would not put up with short trousers for long?

_____

_____

13–15 Read the final paragraph of this passage again. How do you think Nelson Mandela felt at this time? Use evidence from the passage to support your answer.

_____

_____

_____

_____

⬤ 12

E 1

Complete each of these to make a word ending in *ant* or *ent*.

16 reluct_____   **17** irrelev_____   **18** recipi_____

19 immin_____   **20** consist_____   **21** import_____

22 vali_____   **23** ineffici_____   **24** extravag_____

⬤ 9

D 12

Write these sentences as **indirect speech**.

25 'Jake hurt himself at school today,' the teacher informed his mum.

_____

26 'It looks like it might snow,' giggled Lena excitedly.

_____

27 'What time is the match?' Rory enquired.

_____

28 'The police are investigating my missing bike,' Sam informed her class.

_____

4

Use each of these words in a short passage debating whether your school should recycle more than just paper.

C 4

    evidence   furthermore   conclusion   summary   predict

29–33

_____

_____

_____

_____

_____

5

D 10

Write the following **abbreviations** in full.

34 NZ _____

35 approx _____

36 HGV _____

37 mm _____

38 VIP _____

39 TV _____

40 RIP _____

7

Write two sentences, one with three commas separating words in a list and the other with two commas used as a slight pause or break between parts in a sentence.

D 4

41–43 _____

_____

_____

44–45 _____

_____

5

Match each word with its correct word class.

litter   hate   it   masterful   scatter   faintly   because

46 abstract noun _____

47 adverb _____

48 verb _____

49 collective noun _____

50 conjunction _____

51 adjective _____

52 pronoun _____

7

State whether each of these sentences has an **active** or **passive** verb.

53 The wind blew Mr Tomkin's hat off. _____

54 Tuhil caught a huge fish. _____

55 The rain soaked the children walking home from school. _____

56 Hannah was stung by the wasp. _____

57 Jacob jumped off the climbing frame. _____

58 Water spurted from the burst pipe. _____

59 The steaks had been eaten by the dog. _____

7

The words below are spelt incorrectly. Rewrite them correctly.

60 relevent _____   **61** consciance _____

62 mischevous _____   **63** begining _____

64 completly _____   **65** hindrence _____

66 conveniance _____   **67** unnecesary _____

8

Add a **clause** with a **conjunction** to each of these main clauses.

D 2

68 The horse galloped across the field _____

_____

69 The waiter tripped holding two plates of food _____

_____

70 The baby slept peacefully _____

_____

71 Poppy finally finished her book _____

_____

72 At last the audience were seated _____

_____

5

Complete the following **similes**.

C 4

73 As quiet as a _____.

74 As strong as an _____.

75 As dry as _____.

76 As cold as _____.

77 As fit as a _____.

5

Rewrite this passage correctly.

D 5

78–95 what are you doing looking in my bag i asked

is it yours ben sneered i was wondering what my MP3 player was doing in it

i stared in disbelief

_____

_____

_____

_____

_____

18

Underline the unstressed vowel sound in each word.

96 e n t r a n c e   **97** d i c t i o n a r y

98 f r i g h t e n i n g   **99** h i s t o r y

100 d i e s e l

5

Now go to the Progress Chart to record your score!   Total   100

Paper 8

Mma Ramotswe runs the No. 1 Ladies' Detective Agency in Africa. She is the only female private detective in Botswana.

As Mr Patel spoke, the door to his study, which had been closed behind them when they had entered, opened and a woman came into the room. She was a local woman and she greeted Mma Ramotswe politely in Setswana before offering her a tray on which various glasses of fruit juice were set. Mma Ramotswe chose a glass of guava juice and thanked the servant. Mr Patel helped himself to orange juice and   5
then impatiently waved the servant out of the room with his stick, waiting until she had gone before he continued to speak.

'I have spoken to her about this,' he said. 'I have made it very clear to her. I told her that I don't care what other children are doing – that is their parents' business, not mine. I have made it very clear that she is not to go about the town with boys or   10
see boys after school. That is final.'

He tapped his artificial leg lightly with his walking stick and then looked at Mma Ramotswe expectantly.

Mma Ramotswe cleared her throat. 'You want me to do something about this?' she said quietly. 'Is this why you have asked me here this evening?'   15

Mr Patel nodded. 'That is precisely why. I want you to find out who this boy is, and then I will speak to him.'

Mma Ramotswe stared at Mr Patel. Had he the remotest idea, she wondered, how young people behaved these days, especially at a school like Maru-a-Pula, where there were all those foreign children, even children from the American   20
Embassy and such places? She had heard about Indian fathers trying to arrange marriages, but she had never actually encountered such behaviour. And here was Mr Patel assuming that she would agree with him; that she would take exactly the same view.

'Wouldn't it be better to speak to her?' she asked gently. 'If you asked her who   25
the young man was, then she might tell you.'

Mr Patel reached for his stick and tapped his tin leg.

'Not at all,' he said sharply, his voice becoming shrill. 'Not at all. I have already been asking her for three weeks, maybe four weeks. And she gives no answer. She is dumb insolent.' ...   30

... She looked up. Mr Patel was watching her with his dark eyes, the tip of his walking stick tapping almost imperceptibly on the floor.

'I'll find out for you.' she said. 'Although I must say I don't really like doing this. I don't like the idea of watching a child.'

'But children must be watched!' expostulated Mr Patel. 'If parents don't watch their children, then what happens? You answer that!' 35

'There comes a time when they must have their own lives,' said Mma Ramotswe. 'We have to let go.'

'Nonsense!' shouted Mr Patel. 'Modern nonsense. My father beat me when I was twenty-two! Yes, he beat me for making a mistake in the shop. And I deserved it. 40 None of this modern nonsense.'

Mma Ramotswe rose to her feet.

'I am a modern lady,' she said. 'So perhaps we have different ideas. But that has nothing to do with it. I have agreed to do as you have asked me. Now all that you need to do is to let me see a photograph of this girl, so that I can know who it is I 45 am going to be watching.'

Mr Patel struggled to his feet, straightening the tin leg with his hands as he did so.

'No need for a photograph,' he said. 'I can produce the girl herself. You can look at her.'

Mma Ramotswe raised her hands in protest. 'But then she will know me,' she 50 said. 'I must be able to be unobserved.'

'Ah!' said Mr Patel. 'A very good idea. You detectives are very clever men.'

'Women,' said Mma Ramotswe.

Mr Patel looked at her sideways, but said nothing. He had no time for modern ideas.

As she left the house, Mma Ramotswe thought: He has four children; I have 55 none. He is not a good father this man, because he loves his children too much – he wants to own them. You have to let go. You have to let go.

Extract from *The No. 1 Ladies' Detective Agency* by Alexander McCall Smith

Underline the correct answers.

1 What drinks do we know were on offer to Mma Ramotswe?

   (orange juice only, guava juice only, orange and guava juice)

2 What was Mr Patel asking Mma Ramotswe to do?

   (follow his son, follow his daughter, follow a group of children)

3 Mr Patel had an artificial body part. Which part was it?

   (leg, arm, hand)

3

Answer these questions.

4 Why would Mma Ramotswe think that foreign children at Mr Patel's daughter's school would make a difference to her behaviour?

   _____

5–6 What is the meaning of the words 'insolent' (line 30) and 'imperceptibly' (line 32)?

   _____

   _____

7 Why do you think Mr Patel felt that '... children must be watched!' (line 35)?

_____

_____

8–9 Explain whether Mma Ramotswe agreed with Mr Patel about children needing to be watched. Use evidence from the passage to support your answer.

_____

_____

10 Why did Mr Patel's voice become 'shrill' (line 28)?

_____

11 Why didn't Mma Ramotswe want to meet Mr Patel's daughter?

_____

12–13 Using evidence from the passage, discuss Mma Ramotswe's feelings towards Mr Patel.

_____

_____

14 Why did Mr Patel say 'You detectives are very clever men' to Mma Ramotswe?

_____

15 Look again at the last paragraph. Why does the author repeat the last line?

_____

◯ 12

D 5

Circle the letters in the passage that should be capitals.

16–27 'how long until we get to uncle ron's house?' groaned simon.

'not long now. take a left down tiffany street and then we are there,' answered his dad.

they had been cycling for the last two hours and the novelty of the ride had begun to wear off. the newspaper article 'getting fit' had been right, maybe it would be better to do it in short manageable cycle rides!

◯ 12

Using a word from each column write seven **compound words**.

28–34   table   out

           data   teacher

           school   being

           utter   cloth

           check   most

           red   base

           well   head

_____ _____ _____

_____ _____ _____

_____

7

Add a different **conjunction** to each sentence.

35 The stars glistened in the sky _____ the clouds hid them from view.

36 Excitement welled up inside Hannah _____ she got closer to the Queen.

37 Rolf ate his sandwiches _____ it was still too early for lunch.

38 Fran was cross with herself _____ she forgot her swimming costume.

39 Since Rashid broke his leg he still couldn't run _____ he could walk.

40 Mum wondered _____ her washing would dry.

6

Write the **singular** form of these words.

41 atlases   _____   42 syllabi   _____

43 emergencies   _____   44 runways   _____

45 speeches   _____   46 larvae   _____

6

Add a **clause** or **phrase** to each sentence.

47 It took several minutes before they realised where they were.

_____

_____

48 The thought of it terrified the giant.

_____

_____

49 The bird crashed into the closed window.

_____

_____

50 The teacher's explanation confused Kelly even more!

_____

_____

4

Write seven **synonyms** for the word _nice_.

D 9

51–57 _____   _____   _____

_____   _____   _____

_____

7

Underline the correct **verb** form in each sentence.

D 6

58 There (was/were) time to get home before our friends arrived.

59 Marianne (is/are) comfortable in her bed.

60 The dogs (was/were) chasing after the rabbit.

61 There (is/are) a knock at the door.

62 Tim and Sally (is/are) best friends.

5

Draw a line (/) every time a new line should have been started in the following dialogue.

D 3

63–69 'Good-bye,' called the zoo keeper. 'Don't come back next time a lion escapes!' 'Wow!' smiled Meena. 'I didn't think we were going to get out alive.' 'Me neither,' said Rudi. 'What was the scariest moment, Rudi?' 'When you slipped over as the lion started running towards us!' giggled Rudi. 'Mine too!' 'Let's go home and tell your mum.' 'She'll never believe us!'

D 12

7

Write each word in a **metaphor**.

C 4

70 clouds _____

71 snow _____

72 waterfall _____

73 bull _____

74 dew _____

75 quilt _____

6

E 2

Write a word that has the same pronunciation as each of these words.

76 brought _____

77 plough _____

78 rough _____

79 nought _____

80 though _____

81 thorough _____

Write two more *ough* words that have a different pronunciation to all of the ough words in 76–81.

82–83 c_____   th_____

8

E 1

Write in each gap *to*, *too* or *two*.

84–86 It is time _____ take the _____ dogs for a walk

_____ the park.

87–88 He's not _____ well today so I'm taking him _____ the doctor's.

89–90 I think we should start _____ cook the _____ fish on the BBQ.

91–93 I'll have _____ undo _____ trouser buttons _____ feel

comfortable because I've eaten _____ much

10

E 2

Add a different **prefix** to each of these words.

94 _____caution

95 _____construe

96 _____front

97 _____connect

98 _____patriate

99 _____education

100 _____normal

7

Now go to the Progress Chart to record your score!   Total 100

49

Sally Thomas walked from Land's End (the south-west tip of England) to John O'Groats (the most northern point of mainland Scotland). Sally's son was suffering from leukaemia and while in hospital with him she spotted a photograph pinned up on a noticeboard.

'Well done Finlay!' read the caption beneath the picture of an ex-leukaemia patient who had ridden an ancient bike from Land's End to John O'Groats, thereby raising several thousand pounds for leukaemia research. I decided there and then that I too would make this journey, though on foot rather than bicycle. I decided that I would do it whatever the outcome of Jim's illness; if he survived, it would be a thanksgiving, and if not, funds raised would contribute towards research aimed at eliminating this cruel and devastating disease.   5

Sally started her walk on the first anniversary of Jim's death. It took her three and a half months to complete. Her family joined her for the last day.

Keiss to John O'Groats   10

Last night all that was missing was little Dan, though I did talk to him on the phone. I was so excited when they all arrived that I kept thinking I'd finished the journey, and so one of my first thoughts was, 'I must ring Dan!'

It was wonderful to see them all. I'd seen the car coming over the horizon from my bedroom window and so was waiting by the side of the road when they arrived.   15 And then there was a peculiar moment when nothing seemed to happen. There was a lull, and I thought, 'Why don't they get out of the car?' It can only have been for a split second, but it seemed to last forever. I suppose it was a distortion of time such as you hear people describe when they're about to experience a car crash or similar – moments of danger or high emotion, when 'time stood still.' I've never experienced it before. But they got out eventually, beaming and smiling, and then we were all kissing and hugging each other in the quiet, dusty road outside the Sinclair Bay Hotel, and I shall never forget it. They thought I looked thin and I thought they looked wonderful! We had a lovely meal together, everybody talking at the same time, and I've no notion of what we ate. 20 ... 25

And how lovely to set out all together this morning, me without a care in the world! (Still carrying my pack though, emptied of some of its contents. I wouldn't let them carry it for me on the last day!) Michael, David and Tam accompanied me all the way and Berwyn did a bit of sightseeing in Wick and then parked the car in John O'Groats and walked back out to meet us. It was so good to be walking with them on what I still couldn't quite believe was the last day. It seemed quite normal, though I did feel a bit light-headed and couldn't concentrate at all. It was a main road all the way of course but there was hardly any traffic, and we fair skipped along, scrutinising the horizon for our first sight of the sea *ahead*. 30

At last there it was, the sea in front of us, and the first of many signs saying JOHN O'GROATS. We took lots of pictures, draping ourselves around the signs, and walked the last few hundred yards to The End. It's far nicer here than in Land's End with its theme park and commercial tat. John O'Groats is just a big hotel, the sea, and a few small souvenir shops selling lots of postcards ... we all milled around talking and laughing in friendly and slightly embarrassed fashion on this unique, never-to-be-repeated occasion. What an extraordinary day! And how happy I am to be going home tomorrow! 35 ... 40

Extract from *A Walk for Jim* by Sally Thomas

Underline the correct answers.

1 Why did Sally walk from Land's End to John O'Groats?

(to visit her son, to raise funds for leukaemia research, to get fit)

2 Who completed the final day's walking with Sally?

(Berwyn/David/Tam, Michael/Dan/Tam, Michael/David/Tam)

3 What did Sally not like about Land's End?

(its rocky seaside, its theme park, its lack of shops)

3

Answer these questions.

4 Why did Sally think she '... must ring Dan!' (line 13)?

_____

5 Describe in your own words what is meant by 'when time stood still' (line 20).

_____

6 Why did time stand still for Sally?

_____

7 Why did Sally set out 'without a care in the world'?

_____

8–9 Write down the words from the passage that mean:

A temporary period of inactivity.   _____

Looking at carefully.   _____

10–12 Using evidence from the passage describe how Sally felt on completing her journey.

_____

_____

_____

13–15 How would you describe the sort of person Sally is? Give reasons for your answer.

_____

_____

_____

⬤ 12

D 6

Change each of the **nouns** in bold to the infinitive of the **verb**.

Example: He was good at **multiplication**.   to multiply

16 She saw the **advertisement** on television.   _____

17 The **departure** of the train was delayed.   _____

18 The '*Flight* of the Bumble Bee' is a popular piece of music.   _____

19 The **applause** lasted for several minutes.   _____

20 The story reached an interesting **conclusion**.   _____

⬤ 5

Write these in the possessive case, i.e. with an apostrophe.

Example: the bone of the dog   *the dog's bone*

D 5

21 the hats of the girls   _____

22 the spires of the churches   _____

23 the home of Lilia   _____

24 the computer of James   _____

25 the bike of his friend   _____

26 the scissors of the teacher   _____   6

Using the words provided, plus two **verbs** and two **adjectives** of your own, make three sentences.

D 6

27–30 The   girl   towards   the   horse

_____

_____

31–34 The   kite   in   the   sky

_____

_____

35–38 Monty   the   dog   on   the   man

_____

_____   12

Write a **definition** for each of these words.

39 unfurnished   _____

40 dejected   _____

41 courteous   _____

42 spectator   _____

43 assisted   _____

44 endeavour   _____

45 resemble   _____   7

Underline the correct **homophone**.

46 The doctor's (practise, practice) is in Warwick Road.

47 They (practise, practice) their judo.

48 The (principal, principle) of the college had taught abroad.

49 It was a matter of (principal, principle) that he should write the letter.

50 Where is (their, there) rabbit?

51 I put it over (their, there).

52 The (coarse, course) of the river meanders through the field.

53 The material she used was very (coarse, course).

8

Add the correct double letters to create a word.

rr   ll   tt   nn   gg

54 omle _____ e

55 mi _____ ow

56 sha _____ ow

57 fla _____ el

58 a _____ ive

59 qua _____ el

60 go _____ le

61 stru _____

Add the missing colons and semicolons to these sentences.

62 It's snowing I'm so excited.

63–66 People enjoy summer for a number of reasons it's warm they enjoy doing things outside they can have BBQs it stays light late into the evening.

67 We have two types of tree in our garden beech and oak.

6

Match, with a line, the Cockney rhyming slang with its meaning.

68 lump of lead   hair

69 skin and blister   telephone

70 frog and toad   head

71 mince pies   money

72 sugar and honey   road

73 dog and bone   eyes

74 Barnet Fair   sister

7

Add a suitable helper **verb** to each of these **conditional** sentences (when one thing depends on something else).

D 6

75 I _____ ring when I get home if my mum lets me.

76 Should it rain, we _____ buy an umbrella.

77 I _____ do anything unless I hear from you.

78 I _____ like to go swimming, providing it doesn't rain.

79 Your purse _____ be stolen if you leave the car unlocked.

5

Write a **synonym** for the words in bold.

D 9

80 They went on holiday **each year**.   _____

81 Sue goes there quite **often**.   _____

82 She **was sorry** that she had been naughty. _____

83 Tom **made up his mind** to go to the cinema. _____

84 The **people who had been watching** clapped
loudly when the play ended.   _____

85 The **people at the church service** listened
attentively to the vicar's sermon.   _____

86 **Now and then** we go to the cinema.   _____

7

Write the **superlative** form of the **adjective** on the left.

87 **clever**   That is the _____ answer of all.

88 **poor**   The _____ families live there.

89 **bad**   They reported the _____ gale for ten years.

90 **ugly**   She was the _____ of the sisters.

91 **red**   My apple is the _____ one I have ever seen.

92 **generous**   Mum is the _____ person I know.

93 **good**   That is the _____ conker I have played with.

94 **curious**   Alice thought it was the _____ thing she'd seen.   8

Underline the **diminutives**.

95–100	model	bull	owlet	fireplace	lioness
	duckling	hare	gander	piglet	dog
	lambkin	magazine	statuette	eaglet	

6

Now go to the Progress Chart to record your score!   Total   100

She picked herself up, and stared about her. Somebody had chopped a long hole in the cellar ceiling; ragged ends of lath and plaster hung, lit by light trickling down from the dining room above.

Bemused, she heard the siren sound the long, unbroken note of the all-clear. She wished they would make their minds up. She climbed the stairs feeling very weary; *5* the cat kept on rubbing against her, as if wanting to be petted. It nearly tripped her up; she yelled at it angrily.

She forced back the dining-room door, which seemed to have swung to. And stood unable to move.

The windows were gone; the curtains were blowing out through the jagged edges, *10* tangling and tearing themselves. But, more amazingly, the dining-room table lay tilted together in two halves; somebody had chopped it in two. All the silver she had been cleaning lay in the valley in the middle, knives and forks like a shoal of shining fish. On top lay a battered chunk of metal, torn into a kind of silver lace. She had to pick it up before she recognised her coffee-pot. She only recognised *15* it by the handle ... There was a long hole in her carpet, with the darkness showing underneath. The musty smell in the cellar came up to her, with the acrid smell of spilt 'Silvo'. The wall was covered with great pale stars where the plaster had burst out through dangling strips of her best striped Regency wallpaper ...

What had done it? *20*

Then she realised that whatever had done it had passed straight through the spot where she had been standing cleaning the silver. But for the cat ...

Where *was* the cat? Was it hurt?

But it came walking sedately out of the hall, sniffed the wreckage carefully, then sat down and began to wash its shoulder. 25

She remembered the milkman. She ran outside. There was the same long deep kind of hole running across the lawn from a narrow gap in the privet hedge. There were little silver mushrooms scattered all over the lawn. She absently bent and picked one up. It was very heavy for its size. She put it in the pocket of her pinafore. She only realised later that it was a machine-gun bullet, flattened from hitting the 30 brickwork of the bay window.

The milkman was not where he had fallen. He was further up the road, bending over his horse, among a little crowd of people who were gathering. She could see the horse's head and neck, sticking out, through their legs. The head was moving, trying to lift itself ... 35

Slowly, she walked up to the little crowd. She was terrified of what she would see, so she kept her head down. The surface of the road was pitted with a long line of little holes that led straight as an arrow to her fence, her garden, her dining room. Dozens of the little silver mushrooms ...

She reached the back of the crowd; saw their legs. Heard the milkman sobbing, 40 saying things between sobs.

'She's the best horse I ever had. She knew her own way back to the stable. Oh, God, fetch a vet somebody. I can't bear watching her suffer ...'

Mrs Smiley just stood, feeling weary beyond belief. Back turned to the crowd and the terrible breathing of the dying horse. Staring at the tea-roses peeping over 45 Mr Marshall's fence, the same as they did every year.

Rough hands grabbed her by the arms.

'Thank Christ you're safe!'

She knew who it was before she looked up. She felt so upset about the milkman and his horse that she nearly fell against him and wept. But one did not cry in the street. 50

Extract from *Blitzcat* by Robert Westall

Underline the correct answers.

    1 What had Mrs Smiley been doing?

      (cleaning the silver, laying the table, feeding the cat)

    2 What were the little silver mushrooms?

      (ornaments she had been cleaning, a type of fungi, bullets)

Answer these questions.

3–6 In your own words, describe what the story is about. Use three pieces of evidence from the passage to support your answer.

_____

_____

_____

_____

7 Why was Mrs Smiley 'unable to move' (line 9)?

_____

8 Identify a **simile** in the first half of the passage.

_____

9 What does the word 'pitted' mean in line 37?

_____

10 Mrs Smiley yelled at her cat on line 7, yet a little while later was worried about where the cat was. Why do you think she reacted like this?

_____

11 Copy the line that shows that Mrs Smiley had been in danger.

_____

12 There is a sentence in this passage that highlights to the reader that despite everything, 'life goes on'. Which sentence is this?

_____

13–15 Describe the way that Mrs Smiley reacts to the situation she finds herself in. Include two pieces of evidence from the passage to support your answer.

_____

_____

_____

13

D 11

Write the **root word** in each word.

16 signature _____

17 hopefully _____

18 statement _____

19 doubtful _____

59

20 decoration	_____	21 laziness	_____
22 instantaneous	_____	23 extension	_____

Add the missing apostrophes.

24–25 Im sorry were going to be late.

26 Liz fed Aimees ducks.

27 Wheres the party?

28 The dogs coats were muddy and wet.

29–31 Lets hide Jakes homework here, hell never find it.

In each space write an appropriate preposition.

32 Mrs Griffiths sat _____ Nina and Tahir to stop them talking.

33 Laith hid _____ the stage curtains, afraid to go on.

34 I stood _____ the platform waiting for the train.

35 The deer ran back _____ the woods.

36 If you keep rolling sweets _____ your mouth they dissolve slowly.

37 The keys fell _____ the radiator and the wall.

38 Lucy got dressed _____ her insect costume, ready for the party.

Write the feminine of each of these words.

39 baron	_____	40 nephew	_____
41 billy-goat	_____	42 drake	_____
43 duke	_____	44 stag	_____

Write a noun phrase about each of these nouns.

45 a horse _____

46 the moon _____

47 a film _____

48 the wind _____

Rewrite each word, adding the missing silent letter so that each word is spelt correctly.

E 2

49 autum _____

50 kichen _____

51 hankerchief _____

52 sutlety _____

53 salm _____

54 sience _____

55 rench _____

56 colum _____

8

Write these words in reverse **alphabetical order**.

inseparable   insinuate   insistent   inscription   insincere   insensitive

57 (1) _____

58 (2) _____

59 (3) _____

60 (4) _____

61 (5) _____

62 (6) _____

6

Rewrite the passage, separating the words correctly and adding the missing capital letters and punctuation.

D 5

63–89

whoistherecriedstevenputtinghisheadoutofhisbedroomwindowitsmikestevenwhatdoyou

wantheaskedsadiehasfallenfromtheswingscanyouaskyourdadtocomeasquicklyas

possiblesheneedsadoctortocheckherleg

_____

_____

_____

_____

_____

_____

_____

_____

27

Add the missing commas to these sentences.

D 4

90–91 Every afternoon as they were coming home from school Mina and Toby used to play by the banks of the river.

92 It was a lovely large garden with soft green grass.

5

93–94 High above the city on a tall column stood the statue of Nelson.

E 2

Write two words that begin with each of these hyphenated **prefixes**.

95–96 off-   _____ _____

97–98 non-   _____ _____

6

99–100 re-   _____ _____

Now go to the Progress Chart to record your score!   Total ⃝ 100

Progress Chart · English 10–11⁺ years Book 2

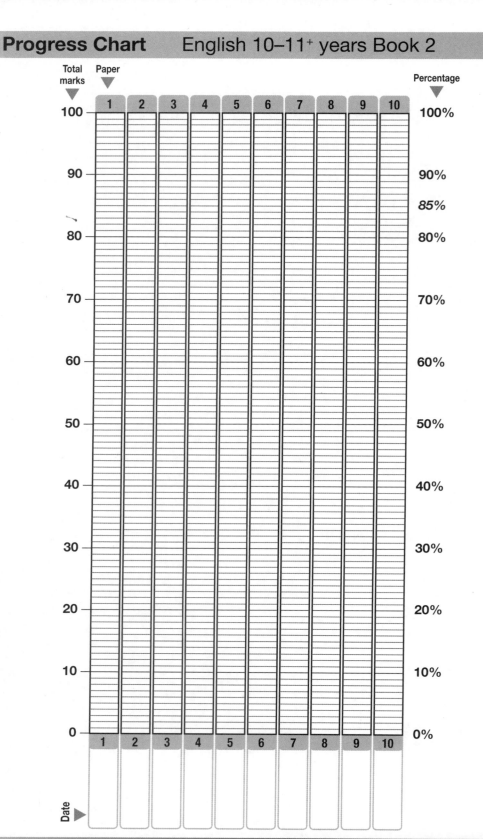

When you've finished the book use the Next Step Planner